Old Sturbridge Village
Cookbook

Old Sturbridge Village Cookbook

Authentic Early American Recipes for the Modern Kitchen

edited by Caroline Sloat

Old Saybrook, Connecticut

**Manufactured in the United States of America
First Edition/Sixth Printing**

Cover and book design by Barbara Marks
Illustrations by Cynthia Dias-Reid
Photographs by Robert S. Arnold
Photographs on bottom of pages 234 and 235
by Donald F. Eaton

**Library of Congress Cataloging in Publication Data
Main entry under title:**

Old Sturbridge Village cookbook.

  Recipes adapted from The American frugal housewife (1829) by Lydia Maria Child.
  Includes bibliographical references and index.
  1. Cookery, American—Massachusetts. I. Sloat, Caroline. II. Child, Lydia Maria Francis, 1802-1880. American frugal housewife. III. Old Sturbridge Village.
TX715.0438   1984   641.59744   84-47762
ISBN 0-87106-885-9
ISBN 0-87106-941-5 (pbk.)

Contents

Introduction

Hearth Cookery

Common Cooking

Vegetables

Herbs

Puddings

Common Pies

Common Cakes

Bread, Yeast, &c.

Preserves, &c.

Appendix

Index

Introduction

I
The American Frugal Housewife

"The true economy of housekeeping is simply the art of gathering up all the fragments, so that nothing be lost." This is how Lydia Maria Child introduced *The American Frugal Housewife*, a book of recipes and forthright advice on household management, first published in Boston in 1829. She wrote her book because she felt that despite "the great variety of cookery books already in the market (she) did not know of one suited to the wants of the middling class in our own country." Her perception was an accurate one, for thousands of households responded by purchasing copies of her book in the next twenty years. And when young women left home to work in the textile factories, they sent the book home to their mothers with their first earnings. Indeed, a whole generation of New England cooks relied on Mrs. Child's emphatic opinions about careful household management.

Mrs. Child's goal was to provide the homemaker, whether the wife of a farmer or artisan, with ways "to avoid waste." Time was to be used profitably by each family member and so were materials. Mrs. Child told her readers how to take care of their new furniture and carpets, and included tips on health care and grooming. But most of the advice in her book relates to economical techniques for cooking and preserving foods. The book answers clearly and well the questions of how early Americans prepared their food and what they ate.

The American Frugal Housewife spoke so eloquently to the households of the early nineteenth century, it is an important source for learning about hearth and home in the early years of the new American republic. Mrs. Child's book is used to guide the reconstruction and interpretation of domestic life and cooking at Old Sturbridge Village, the living history museum of early-nineteenth-century New England life, located in Sturbridge, Massachusetts. More than half a million visitors each year watch the costumed staff of Old Sturbridge Village prepare and cook Mrs. Child's recipes in houses restored to the period. Many visitors have participated in hands-on cooking activities during their museum visit or as a part of special programs offered. "Where can I find these recipes?" is the question frequently heard.

The recipes provided in the *Old Sturbridge Village Cookbook* are based on the experiences of the Village staff in finding out just how the recipes in Mrs. Child's book should be prepared, and how the results should taste.

Mrs. Child wrote about the kind of cooking she knew best — hearth cooking. There was just about no alternative in her time. Cookstoves were still a novelty and many did not work well. Her directions call for using the fireplace, cooking in hanging pots, heating coals to draw onto the hearth to use the Dutch oven, and heating and using the brick bake-oven. Using Mrs. Child's instructions, hearthside cooks at Old Sturbridge Village were able to perfect these techniques. Each recipe was prepared at the hearth or brick oven. With the results as a guide, the recipes were then prepared again, this time at a stove, to reproduce those same results. Thus verified, the recipes appear in this book in three ways: in their original form as they appeared in Mrs. Child's book, in a variation adapted to stove cooking, and again with hearth-cooking instructions. These authentic recipes are presented here to provide today's cooks with an overview of cooking practices in the early 1800s, along with actual recipes from the period that can be produced in the modern kitchen, either at the stove or at the hearth and brick oven.

II
Early New England Cookbooks

Until *The American Frugal Housewife* was published, most of the cookbooks for sale in New England were English or American editions of English books. American house-wives must have had some problems using these books, which generally ignored common American foods, included others that were not readily available in rural New England and assumed that the food was cooked and served by a staff working in a kitchen from which they could "send up" the meals. As recipes were found to be appealing, however, they were gradually incorporated into versions adapted for the American market or copied by New England women for their personal recipe collections.

The Frugal Housewife and Compleat Woman Cook by Sus-annah Carter enjoyed great success in Britain and several American editions. The first American edition published in 1772 included illustrations engraved by Paul Revere. Edi-tions which appeared after 1800 included "an appendix con-taining new receipts adapted to the American mode of cooking." A few of these receipts or recipes, as we call them today, even found their way into *American Cookery*, pub-lished in Hartford, Connecticut, in 1796 by Amelia Sim-mons. Little more is known of Simmons than her own description as an "American orphan." The full title of her book doubles as a table of contents: *American Cookery or the Art of Dressing Viands, Fish, Poultry, and Vegetables and the best modes of making pastes, puffs, pies, tarts, puddings, custards and preserves and all kinds of cakes from the imperial plumb to*

plain cake, adapted to this country and all grades of life. American Cookery was reprinted in many different editions for the
next forty years. Some of these were credited to Simmons
and others were not. The book was popular because it appears to have been written from actual experience in a New
England kitchen using ingredients that were commonly
available. It includes recipes for johnnycakes and flapjacks
using cornmeal, for pumpkin and squash pies, as well as molasses gingerbread. None of these foods had been known in
Old England, but all became standard fare for New Englanders. Along with her original recipes, however, Mrs. Simmons appears to have had a copy of Carter's *Frugal Housewife*
for reference, since some of the recipes are remarkably
similar.

Another family of Anglo-American cookbooks is de-
scended from Maria Rundell's *A New System of Domestic
Cookery.* The third London edition was published in 1808, a
year after the first American edition had been published in
Boston. Between 1807 and 1823 when the title was changed,
ten American editions appeared. Retitled *The Experienced
American Housekeeper or Domestic Cookery,* it began a new
life, published first in New York and then in Hartford, Connecticut. The recipes calling for ingredients more readily
available in England remained unchanged despite its claims
that it was "adapted to the use of private families throughout
the United States."

Versions of Simmons and Rundell were current when
Mrs. Child wrote *The American Frugal Housewife,* although
she was apparently unaware of Carter's *Frugal Housewife*
when she titled her book. So subsequent editions of Mrs.
Child's book noted that "it became necessary to change the
title" to include the word American "because there is an *English* work of the same name, not adapted to the wants of this
country." What Mrs. Child felt that America needed was
"information . . . of a common kind . . . such as the majority
of young housekeepers do not possess and such as they cannot obtain from cookery books." It was designed to appeal to

6

other women who, like herself, had to stretch limited resources into an appearance of elegance and plenty. She had filled her book with down-to-earth advice about running a house. For the city resident, the foods could be purchased in the markets. For the country dweller, the foods were grown in the fields and gardens of New England farms or village houses, or like cranberries and huckleberries, were growing wild. Other foods, flour and raisins, for example, were for sale in the country stores of the region.

The recipes, tending to be practical and economical, are grouped under the headings "Common Cooking," "Vegetables," "Herbs," "Puddings," "Common Pies," "Common Cakes," "Bread, Yeast," and "Preserves, . . ." This order of recipes has been followed in the *Old Sturbridge Village Cookbook*. Perhaps the simplicity of Mrs. Child's recipes made her advice on other subjects more palatable. She gave advice on polishing furniture, simple remedies, and on raising children. She shared her opinion that children should not be allowed to "romp away" their time at play, but could be given tasks like picking berries or simple household chores that would teach them the skills they would eventually need for keeping house for themselves.

By the time the cookbook was written, Mrs. Child was well established as an author on New England subjects based on her own experiences. Until she was twelve, she lived with her parents in Medford, just outside Boston, where her father was a baker. After her mother died in 1814, her father broke up housekeeping, sending young Maria to live with her older sister who was already married. Maria moved to Norridgewock, Maine, to help her sister with the new babies as they came along and to entertain many visitors during the year. Mary Preston's husband was a lawyer and as Norridgewock was a county seat, it bustled with lawyers while courts were in session. All these out-of-towners boarded with townspeople for weeks at a time, adding to the work of the household. So, along with her schooling and private reading, Maria had a practical education in household management.

In her late teens, Maria left her sister's home to become a teacher in a district school in another Maine town. She returned to the Boston area soon after her elder brother, Convers Francis, married and settled as the Unitarian minister in Watertown. He invited her to join his household. For something to do, she opened a school for girls and began to write. Her first book, *Hobomok*, a novel about New England life, was published in 1824 and was so successful she began work on another. *The Rebels* was published the following year. By this time she was in her early twenties, an established teacher and writer. She had also made the acquaintance of an idealistic young lawyer, David Lee Child.

After their marriage in October 1828, it became apparent that the income from Maria's writing was vital for their support. She drew on her own experience to write several volumes of domestic advice, including *The Mother's Book* and *The Girls' Own Book,* as well as *The American Frugal Housewife*. With her experience helping her sister and her knowledge of young women and philosophy of education, developed in her years of school teaching, she turned to what she knew best. Later she became editor of *The Juvenile Miscellany*, a successful periodical for young people. When she became caught up in the antislavery movement, many parents felt that her ideas were not a good influence on their youngsters, and she lost many friends and subscribers. Her efforts toward the freeing of the slaves dominated most of her writing in the second quarter of the nineteenth century. However, even though she wrote only one cookbook, it went through so many revisions for its many editions that it made her name literally a household word.

At first, however, she had to persevere to find a printer willing to produce the book. It was rejected repeatedly "on account of the variety of cookbooks already on the market." But Mrs. Child would not accept that for a reason. Finally, she managed to convince one publisher that her book was written for a special audience. She was right, for by 1850, the thirty-second edition was published. In that quarter century, many other cookbooks appeared, too. One of them was *The New England Economical Housekeeper* published in Worcester, Massachusetts, in 1845. If imitation is the sincerest form of flattery, then it is clear that Mrs. Esther Allen Howland, its author, admired Mrs. Child's book. Mrs. Howland began by paraphrasing the title, substituting *New England* for *American, Economical* for *Frugal,* and *Housekeeper* for *Housewife.* She also included a number of Mrs. Child's recipes without giving credit. There were many more recipes, too, reflecting the passage of twenty years and the evolution of cooking techniques. Her husband was a prominent printer in Worcester, and he must have been delighted with the public response to his wife's book. The first edition of 1,500 copies sold out in fifteen weeks, and new editions followed in rapid succession.

Fifty years later, at the end of the century, Mrs. Child's book surfaced again, this time in a curious disguise. By then, the book had been superseded as a standard by many others, including the indomitable Fannie Farmer's *The Boston Cooking School Cook Book.* A group of ladies in Deerfield, Massachusetts, borrowed liberally from *The American Frugal Housewife,* added a fancy new subtitle and some antiquarian notes of their own to produce "a guide to domestic cookery as practiced in the Connecticut Valley" entitled *The Pocumtuc Housewife.* It was claimed that the book was based on "original sources" dating from 1805. This was in 1895, and whether or not purchasers of this little volume have known much about its actual origins, it has achieved some popularity and has remained in print benefiting the Parish Guild of the First Church of Deerfield, Massachusetts, through the years.

Most recently, *The American Frugal Housewife* has been made available in a facsimile of the twelfth edition, first published in 1832. The Worthington (Ohio) Historical Society undertook this project. So the original recipes are in print once again, but in the same general and unspecific manner that plagued a young minister's bride in the middle of the nineteenth century. Her cookbook was not apparently *The American Frugal Housewife*, but another one which let her down badly as she tried to become an efficient homemaker and cook in the first months of married life. Her most devastating experience, still memorable years afterwards, was trying to make a chowder. It called for vast amounts of some ingredients, far too much for two people, and pinches of others, which as a bride on a limited budget, she was completely lacking. She reduced the ingredients, compromised on some, built the layers in the kettle, then hung it over the fire. She cooked it twice as long as the cookbook directed and even then, it was still in three layers: uncooked on top, chowder in the middle and burned on the bottom. "After dark that night," she wrote, "the masculine head of the house quietly buried it in a corner of the garden, that the incompetence of his wife, as a cook, might never be discovered and bruited about."[1] The present version seeks to avoid a duplication of such an episode.

Most of the recipes from *The American Frugal Housewife* are presented in this book, which is organized just like the original. Some recipes have been omitted: They called for ingredients that are not commonly available or require techniques that are hardly worth the bother. As a result, there are no recipes for souse, tripe, pigeon or roast pig included. Few today would examine pigeons legs to ascertain their ages before deciding whether to pot, roast or stew them. The directions for the pig were not specific enough: The way to tell how long the whole pig would take to cook is "when the eyes drop out the pig is half done." We also feel that the directions for cooking a calf's head "with the wind-pipe" on were likely to be tried only once, and only by a Village staffer with a very strong stomach. "If it hangs out of the pot while the head is cooking, all the froth will escape through it," we are told. Mrs. Child also gives a variety of recipes for boiled puddings to be cooked in a bag submerged in boiling water. However, she did not give specific descriptions for this technique, and repeated attempts at Village hearths have failed to produce a palatable result. We have come to agree with the woman who wrote a cookbook several years later, who noted emphatically that "there is no way of *boiling* wheat *dough* which can render it fit for food." Mrs. Child noted that her book included nothing fancy; she recommended that "those who can afford to be epicures" should look elsewhere for recipes. Epicureanism figured less significantly than practicability. So leaving out recipes like these left room to include a number that are popular with the staff at Old Sturbridge Village.

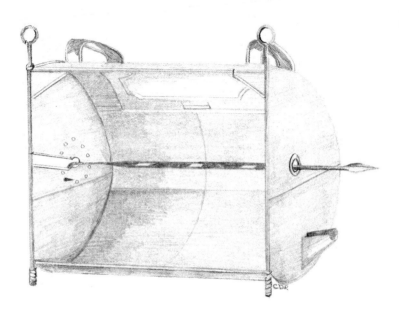

Tin Kitchen

III
New England Cooking

New Englanders were hearty eaters, according to one of her native sons. Calvin Plimpton, of Easton, Massachusetts, said that the region's "food may well be called substantial and the variety and quantity are enough to denote a land of plentiful supply."[2] Calvin Plimpton was not alone in wanting "meat or its equivalent to be served three times a day." He wanted meat, fish, eggs, or oysters served throughout the year, and so each fall he would lay by "a part of a sheep, beef and a barrel of oysters."[3]

When a Vermont farmer took over the operation of the family farm from his ageing parents, he signed a bond for their support promising to provide a specified quantity and variety of food for them. Their annual meat needs were "a healthy merchantable fat hog, weighing 300 pounds, three hundred pounds of good beef, half a barrel of Mackerel No. 2, also the milk and calves of three good cows." In addition, from the fields and gardens, the supplies were to include "rye and Indian meal [corn], potatoes, cyder apples, garden sauce of all kinds and also fruit of all kinds in their season which the farm produces. . . . [From the store should be procured] five bushels of wheat, one pound of green tea, two pounds of bohea tea and ginger, alspice and pepper of each one pound, ten pounds of brown sugar, two pounds of loaf sugar, one gallon of molasses, one of West India rum and two gallons of cider brandy," as well as an unspecified quantity of salt.[4]

Dedicated as it was to economy, *The American Frugal Housewife* gives meat a prominent place among the recipes.

"Common Cooking" is the title of the section devoted to the preparation of meat, poultry, and fish. The recipes include roasting, broiling, and stewing the various cuts of beef, veal, mutton, lamb, pork, and poultry, as well as fish. Stews, hashes, and meat pies also figure, along with the caveat about preparing chopped meat. There is a "great difference in preparing mince meat. . . . It is generally considered nicer to chop meat fine. . . . to be brought upon the table without being mixed with potatoes." Mrs. Child recommended that economy in the use of meat came in careful purchasing for city folk. Cuts that could provide more than one meal were the most economical, even if not the cheapest by the pound. Every cook had to pay attention to the condition of the meat. Whether this meat was being stored fresh in the coolest possible place in hot weather or stored in brine, it should be checked frequently to prevent waste through spoilage.

The New England day traditionally began with a breakfast described as "no evanescent thing." In the country "breakfast is held at an early hour and often by sunrise."[5] The hour was not so early, however, that a lot of cooking could take place, including the baking of fresh bread. Directions for several of the breads include "setting a sponge" or mixing a thin batter with yeast in the evening to allow the first rising overnight in cold weather. The second rising was in the morning while the fire burned to coals for the Dutch oven or in the brick oven for the requisite two hours of preheating.

Mrs. Child's one specific menu suggestion for breakfast is fish cakes. "There is no way of preparing salt fish for breakfast so nice as to roll it up in little balls, after it is mixed with mashed potatoes; dip it into egg and fry it brown," she wrote. In the upper-middle-class household of Judge Joseph Lyman of Northampton, Massachusetts, his daughter recalled that "the breakfast was always simple but abundant, tea and coffee, broiled fish or steak, bread and some kind of pudding for the children to be eaten with milk or cream."[6] The author of *The House Servant's Directory* provided his readers with the ways to do their jobs efficiently and well.

Aside from the cooking of the breakfast, not the focus of this book, the other major preparations included setting the table for cold meat which would be carved at the table and for hot eggs, toast, rolls, butter and cream, as well as tea or coffee.[7] "Boiled beef, when thoroughly done," says another cookbook, "is excellent to eat cold, as a relish for breakfast. The slices should be cut even and very thin."[8] Where supplies of food were plentiful the meal served might consist of "ham, beef, sausages or pork, as well as bread, butter, boiled potatoes, pies, coffee and cider."[9] The aromas of frying meat, fresh bread, and coffee must have brought many a hardworking farmer in from barn chores for breakfast.

Dinner was the major meal of the day, served at 1 P.M. for country families and an hour later in the city. Elegant dinner parties were held in the evening. Ironically, it was the Sunday noon meal that was the exception to the rule of a hot dinner with meat and potatoes followed by some kind of pudding. Many devout families did not do any heavy cooking on the Sabbath, and if they lived at a distance from the meetinghouse, they were unable to return home to eat in the interval between the morning and afternoon services that they had to attend.

In the Lyman household, the main meal of the day was dinner at 1 P.M., "always a joint roast or boiled with plenty of vegetables and few condiments, for Mother thought them unwholesome, good bread and butter and a plain pudding or pie."[10] In contrast, however, the tradition in the home of former President John Adams, described in two separate reminiscences some years apart, varied from the norm. "I well remember the modest dinners at the President's to which I brought a schoolboy's appetite," Josiah Quincy recalled years later. "The pudding generally composed of boiled cornmeal always constituted the first course. This was the custom of the time, it being thought desirable to take the edge off one's hunger before reaching the joint."[11] Despite the customs at the Adams home, many families served hasty pudding at the end of the meal with butter and molasses.

The best-remembered dinner of the year was the Thanksgiving meal, which could last as long as two hours, while the foods cooked during the preceding days made their way to the table. "You began with your chicken pie and your roast turkey. You ate as much as you could, and you then ate what you could of mince pie, squash pie, Marlborough pie, cranberry tart and plum pudding. Then you went to work on the fruits as you could. The use of dried fruits at the table was much more frequent in those days than in these. Dates, prunes, raisins, figs and nuts held a much more prominent place in a handsome dessert."[12] All the food prepared and served was, in the words of one writer, a "noble dinner" and "all are as happy as possible remembering who it is that has given us all these good things."[13]

The last meal of the nineteenth-century day was tea. Between five and six in the evening in country families, bread and butter, sometimes freshly made biscuits, assorted cakes, relishes, and even meats were on the menu. When fresh fruits, like strawberries, were in season, they would be served at this meal. Otherwise, apple sauce, baked apples, other preserves, and pickles made their appearance. "If it was to be a tea-party" at the Lymans, recalled the youngest daughter, "[Mother] had only to order an abundant supply of tea and coffee, with thin slices of bread and butter doubled, sponge cake made by the daughters before breakfast and thin slices of cold tongue or ham."[14] Sewing societies, which met in the afternoons at members' homes, generally did their good work, spent an hour or so socializing over tea, and then adjourned. At one meeting of the Leicester, Massachusetts, sewing society, tea was served with "many accompanyments, though the rule is not to have but two kinds, say bread, buttered, cheese and nut cakes or sponge cake and the rule at the last annual meeting was to separate about 5 and take tea at home."[15]

One cookbook recommended that "common gingerbread and several varieties of the cheap and simple cakes are much better as a part of the evening meal than hot biscuits or even a full supper of cold bread and butter in the winter season, when butter is too heavily salt [too heavily salted for preservation] to be healthful."[16] Tea time was often a hungry time, and in one reminiscence, the family would make "sad havoc among the flapjacks, gingerbread and plumb cakes."[17] In another family "great kettles full of hasty pudding were easily disposed of as 'pudding and milk' and too little remained to serve as fried pudding at breakfast."[18]

If there were evening callers by invitation or by chance, a tray of fancy cakes might be passed around, accompanied by a glass of wine or brandy. If a special party were planned, like an oyster supper or a major birthday party, then there would be a special menu for that. "Such parties are very common in private families of fashionable standing," noted Robert Roberts, author of *The House Servant's Directory*, for the benefit of future generations of household servants. Roberts noted that cards might be played before supper.[19] At John Quincy Adams's eightieth birthday party, there was dancing to precede a "pretty supper, with ices and champagne."[20] Roberts's instructions indicate that tables were to be set with cutlery for eating a selection of hot and cold foods, as well as glasses for wine, champagne, and cold water. And at the end of a long day of eating and drinking, some New Englanders confessed to a glass of brandy or gin with hot water to aid digestion and a good night's sleep.

Flapjacks, spongecakes, boiled beef, broiled fish, bread, and rolls are all among the recipes included in *The American Frugal Housewife*, which makes that book an exciting road map for reading about the nineteenth century. Any time that food is mentioned in a novel or reminiscence of the period, there is a great probability that there is also a recipe in Mrs. Child's book.

Some of the recipes have a story that is not included in *The American Frugal Housewife*, for Mrs. Child did not resort to anecdotes in presenting her recipes. The recipe for Election Cake was, like many of the cakes, a sweetened bread, made with yeast. It was one of those recipes for foods that

Breakfast:

1.

Minced Meat
or Sliced Cold Beef
Eggs
Fried Potatoes
Three-Grain Bread, Butter
Tea, Coffee

2.

Fresh Fruit
or Apple Sauce
Codfish Balls
Toast, Butter
Hasty Pudding, Fried in
Slices, with Molasses
Tea, Coffee

Tea:

*"The common gingerbread and
several varieties of the cheap and
simple cakes . . ."*

Doughnuts
Flapjacks
Sliced Ham or Tongue
Bread and Butter

Oyster Supper:

Oysters
— Broiled, Raw, Escalloped —
Mashed and Browned Potatoes
Light Rolls, Butter
Water, Cider, Wine
A George Pudding
Orange Fool

Refreshments
for the Militia:

*"After the oration came another
national salute, thirteen guns, one
for each of the original states . . .
and then an attack upon the bread
and cheese and rum punch provided
by the committee."*
— Francis M. Thompson, *History of
Greenfield, Shire Town of Franklin County*

Dinner:

"A large joint roast or boiled with plenty of vegetables and few condiments, good bread and butter and a plain pudding or pie."

1.
Roast Veal
Boiled New Potatoes
Asparagus
Beets
Peas
Shortcake, Fresh Strawberries

2.
Beef A La Mode
Stuffing Balls
Mashed Potatoes
String Beans
Pickled Beets
Rice Pudding with Fruit

3.
Chicken Fricassee
Boiled Potatoes
Carrots
Parsnips
Rhubarb Pie

4.
Roast Pork
Boiled Potatoes
Applesauce
Mashed Turnip
Apple Pie

5.
"An Economical Dinner"
Baked Beans with Pork
Indian Pudding

6.
"A Very Economical Dinner"
1 lb. Sausage, Cut in Pieces
Potatoes Fried with Onions
Squash Pie

Thanksgiving Dinner:

Roast Turkey, Stuffed
Chicken Pie
Potatoes
Turnip, Squash, Onions
Gravy
Applesauce, Cranberry Sauce
Flour Bread
Quaking Plum Pudding
with Better Sauce
Mince, Pumpkin,
and Marlborough Pies

figured in people's childhood memories. "Old Election 'Lection Day as we call it" was mourned as a "lost holiday" by the end of the nineteenth century. "It came at the most delightful season, the last of May [when] lilies and tulips were in bloom." As the flowers bloomed and the militia mustered on the green, the children could always count on a snack of the Election Cake which their mother made for the occasion. "It was nothing but a kind of sweetened bread with a slice of egg and molasses on top, but we thought it delicious."[21]

Cherry pie is another recipe without marginal notes. By the time Mrs. Child wrote, Parson Weems's apocryphal story of George Washington had been in print for a generation. Yet there is little or no evidence that cherry pies were eaten in Washington's honor. Rather, a recipe that made the rounds was for a cake said to have been enjoyed by the first president. A version of the recipe that appeared in a New Hampshire newspaper in 1843 noted that "Washington cake was so called because it was a favorite at the table of General Washington."[22]

Implicit in *The American Frugal Housewife* are the assumptions about the sources of food, methods of storage, ways of measuring, and handy substitutes in the larder of households of 150 years ago. Understanding this culture is part of the fun of reading and interpreting the old recipes.

The sources of food were different. Country farmers had to grow their own corn and rye, and depending on the soil, their own wheat, too. The harvested grains were taken to be ground at the local mill, and the year's crop was the year's supply for food, and the seed for the following year. City dwellers relied on the stores to provide flour, and even the stores in rural communities offered wheat from New York State's Genesee Valley after the opening of the Erie Canal in 1825.

Neither refrigeration nor canning were used in households for food storage. Foods had to be eaten in the seasons in which they grew and processed for storage, too. Beans and peas had to be shelled and dried. Other vegetables, particularly cucumbers and cabbages could be pickled in vinegar, flavored with herbs and spices. Pumpkins, squashes, cabbages, and onions had to be stored in a dry place, warm enough without danger of freezing. Small wonder then, that so many root crops were grown in the gardens of the period. Potatoes, turnips, beets, and carrots could be stored in barrels of sand in a root cellar under the house. Young corn could be boiled for eating, but the varieties of corn grown were flint corn, not tender butter and sugar that barely needs steaming. The corn was left in the fields until it dried and hardened, and then it was picked, husked and eventually flailed to remove the kernels from the cob. This grain was then taken to the mill to be ground into cornmeal. "See that your vegetables are neither sprouting nor decaying," was a useful piece of advice for Mrs. Child's readers. "Examine your pickles to see that they are not growing soft and tasteless." One could only hope that the winter's cold would not become so intense that the vegetables stored in the cellar would freeze.

Directions for using meats reflect the practices of a different era when the seasons of the year determined what was available, and whether fresh or preserved. Markets provided fresh meat for city dwellers long before rural farms could abandon their traditional patterns of raising animals and storing the cuts of meat in barrels of brine for the winter. Veal and lamb generally appeared on springtime menus. Chickens and other fowl could be eaten at almost any time in the country, since they could be killed and completely eaten before there was danger of spoilage. Poultry, however, was most available and cheapest in the city markets in the late summer or fall, when they were large enough to withstand a journey along the roads from the country towns where they had been raised.

The records of the country stores indicate that salt fish was purchased in quantity in the summer months. Once upon a time, the beaches of Cape Cod were spread with racks for drying brine-soaked fish brought back from the ocean by the local fishermen. All the salt works on the Cape produced salt for this industry, which in turn provided barrels of dried salt fish for the population of New England. Because this fish was impregnated with so much salt for preservation, Mrs. Child includes very extensive directions for soaking it.

Salted foods were standard in New England diets. Larger animals like pigs and beef cattle were generally slaughtered late in the fall. There were two reasons for the timing. From the farmer's point of view, the animals could be slaughtered before winter snows then freezing made continued grazing impossible and large amounts of hay and grain would be required to carry the livestock through the winter. Secondly, the chilly days of November and December allowed time for cutting up and preparing the meat for storage without its spoiling. Pork and beef were usually cut up and pickled in brine. Sausages would be made, and along with the hams, might be smoked for flavor and keeping qualities. Directions for preparing barrels and brine are given in *The American Frugal Housewife*. Hams had to be pickled in the brine before they could be smoked in either the kitchen chimney or the smokehouse.

Having put the salt into the meat, directions then had to be given for "freshening," or soaking the salt out of the cut to make them ready for cooking. These directions are interesting commentaries on the period diet, but for the most part, can be ignored today.

Another aspect of meat cookery that shows how change has taken place is evidenced by the cooking times for fresh meat which sometimes seem short. This is because the animals used for meat were not improved, or specially bred for their meaty qualities, as they are for commercial use today. When the directions for roasting a lamb state that the whole leg could cook in less than an hour, they refer to a very young lamb of the multipurpose variety standard for raising both wool and meat during the early nineteenth century. Another tradition that no longer survives because of improved breeding is that of serving chicken pie along with the Thanksgiving turkey. Back then, a large turkey weighed about eight pounds, hardly enough to feed a large and festive Thanksgiving family reunion.

More than anything else, perhaps, it is the old way of writing recipes that make them seem most foreign to us today. In many ways, the wording of the early nineteenth-century recipes is like a foreign language. To begin, it was a time before standardized measurements. The cook stopped adding flour to Election Cake when the dough was "soft as it can be and still moulded on a board" or stopped adding cornmeal to hasty pudding "when it is so thick that you stir it with great difficulty." When Mrs. Child was specific she called for flour by the quart or by the cup, only sometimes by the teacupful, which is about three quarters of a cup. Only a handful of flour was needed in Indian cake (corn bread). Liquids were measured in quarts, pints and fractions of pints called gills, pronounced jills. A gill is about half a cup. In Mrs. Child's kitchen, there was no set of standard spoons. She had her tablespoons and teaspoons, which sound familiar enough, but also a dessert spoon and a great spoon, which she favored while cooking.

The leavening agents frequently used for cakes and quick breads included not only beaten eggs, but a trio of strangers in today's kitchen — pearlash, saleratus, and lively emptings. Pearlash, as its name suggests, was a grey color and derived from wood ashes. It worked much like baking powder. Saleratus, like pearlash, was a bicarbonate of potash, which contained more carbon dioxide than pearlash. Baking soda is a good substitute for saleratus in recipes. Lively emptings were a handy substitute for eggs at a time when beer was commonly made at home. The emptings were the yeasty settlings of the beer barrel, what was left when emptying it. In making doughnuts, for example, Mrs. Child recommended that a gill of lively emptings be mixed in with the flour and sugar instead of eggs.

Mrs. Child's book remained popular for so long that it is not surprising that its recipes should be at the heart of the cuisine of the first half of the nineteenth century. Even in 1843, the book was recommended to the brides of New Hampshire. "It is adapted to our country and the habits of our people. . . . Almost, if not quite all other works upon this subject are extravagant and not suited to the plain frugal wife. Mrs. Child in her Frugal Housewife has won unfading laurels in producing that which is calculated to benefit the greatest number."[23]

Notes:

1. Mary A. Livermore, *The Story of My Life* (Hartford, Conn., 1899), pp. 404-6.

2. Samuel G. Goodrich, *A Pictorial Geography of the World* (Boston, 1840), p. 144.

3. Priscilla Robertson, *Lewis Farm: A New England Saga* (Norwood, Mass., c. 1952), pp. 140-41.

4. Dummerston, Vermont, *Deeds*, vol. 8, Clark Rice to Elijah Rice, Jan. 23, 1823.

5. Goodrich, p. 144.

6. Susan I. Lesley, *Recollections of My Mother* (Boston, 1899), p. 417.

7. Robert Roberts, *The House Servant's Directory*, (Boston, 1827), reprint ed., Waltham, Mass., 1977, p. 42.

8. Sarah J. Hale, *The Way to Live Well and Be Well While We Live* (Philadelphia, 1839), p. 41.

9. Goodrich, p. 144.

10. Lesley, p. 419.

11. "The Adamses at Home, 1788-1886," Colonial Society of Massachusetts, vol. 45 (1970), p. 15.

12. Edward E. Hale, *A New England Boyhood* (Boston, 1900), p. 115.

13. Mary E. Dewey, ed., *The Life and Letters of Catharine M. Sedgwick*, (New York, 1872), p. 102.

14. Lesley, p. 421.

15. Journal of Ruth Henshaw Bascom, September 24, 1840, American Antiquarian Society, Worcester, Mass., in *The New-England Galaxy*, vol. 20, no. 3 (Winter 1979), p. 51.

16. Hale, p. 95.

17. "A Newburyport wedding One Hundred and Thirty Years Ago," *Essex Institute Historical Collections*, vol. 87, no. 4, (October, 1951), p. 313.

18. Alice J. Jones, *In Dover on the Charles* (Newport, R.I., 1906), p. 50.

19. Robert Roberts, *The House Servant's Directory*, p. 63.

20. "The Adamses at Home," p. 47.

21. Lucy Larcom, *A New England Girlhood* (Boston, 1889), p. 98.

22. "Washington Cake," *The Farmer's Monthly Visitor* (April 29, 1843), p. 63.

23. "Instruction to Young Women," *The Farmer's Monthly Visitor* (August 31, 1843), p. 119.

Hearth Cookery

Hearth Cookery

Most of us today have not learned hearth cookery at our mother's knee. Nor have cookbook authors of the past made it easy to reconstruct the methods used to cook the recipes in their books. Lydia Maria Child, like the others, did not describe technique at length, rather, she assured her readers that there was no substitute for experience. In a few instances, she does mention the appropriate cooking vessel. When she names a pan for baking, it is seldom possible to match up her statement with objects which are now part of museum collections of cooking equipment.

To cook with any degree of convenience at the hearth, it should be equipped with at least a pair of andirons and a swinging crane, as a minimum. If you must make a choice of cooking pots, a Dutch oven or bake-kettle offers the most flexibility for cooking over the fire and using coals on the hearth. In order to use the brick oven, a metal shovel for removing ashes is most essential, and can be used for that and removing cooked food. However, a peel, a flat wooden shovel with a long handle, is the correct implement for taking cooked food from the oven. If you only have a flat metal shovel, it should be carefully cleaned after use to remove ashes.

Andirons are essential for building a fire, for they provide a base on which to build and provide for the circulation of air into the fire. It is possible to substitute a pair of quarter-split logs for andirons, but they will eventually become part of the fire. Metal andirons will last virtually forever. Early-nineteenth-century probate inventories of even the poorest dwellings include at least one pair of andirons, indicating that they were very common.

In order to hang pots over the fire to boil water, or for more extensive cooking projects, the hearth must be equipped with a mechanism for hanging a pot or kettle. A **crane,** built into the side of the fireplace, provides the most flexible way to suspend the pots, for the cook can swing it over the flames for cooking, and toward the hearth when additions have to be made to the pots or the contents need to be stirred and tasted. To vary the height of the pot, an adjustable hook called a trammel, or one or more S-shaped iron hooks may be used. The distance between the pot and the fire may be adjusted by the placement of the hook on the trammel, or by adding or removing S-hooks.

The making of the first cast-iron cooking pots in Coalbrookdale, England, in the early eighteenth century revolutionized the use of the hearth. Over the years, cast iron has proved itself in cooking situations and continues to have its devotees despite all the innovations in the last 200 years. Laundry, as well as cooking, were among the domestic chores which were aided by having a vessel large enough to be heated directly and safely over a fire. Many of the recipes for preparing meat by boiling it with vegetables call for one of the bulbous, cast-iron pots.

By the early nineteenth century, a variety of cast-iron forms were being used for hearth cooking, in addition to the original three-legged pot which itself was made in many different sizes. The hanging griddle and hanging skillet were both used for frying foods. Both are round, with a semicircular handle. for suspending the pan over the heat.

Another large pot, the **Dutch oven**, is deeper than the skillet but not as deep as the cooking pot. It has three legs, a handle, and a close-fitting lid. The cookbooks of the period are not specific about the possible uses for this piece of equipment. A kettle or stew-kettle is specified for some recipes in the "Common Cooking" section for making chicken stews, in particular. The advantage of the Dutch oven, or bake-kettle, is that it has a lid to cover the stews as they simmer. It is a piece of equipment with a variety of uses as the alternative name, bake-kettle, implies. It can be heated and used to bake pies, biscuits, and puddings instead of firing the brick oven. To use it for baking, the pot and lid should be preheated in front of the fire. When the food is ready to be cooked, it should be placed inside the Dutch oven, which is then covered with the heated lid. It is placed over a bed of glowing coals drawn out from the fire, and more coals are shoveled on top of the lid. If the coals are not hot enough to cook the contents during the average baking time given in the recipe, fresh hot coals can be added so that cooking will continue.

A **spider** is another piece of cast-iron cooking equipment for use on the hearth. It is like a frying pan with legs that stand over a bed of coals. Meat is broiled on a gridiron. The iron bars which support the meat resemble the markings on a football field. It also has feet and a long handle to simplify its use. A **wafer iron** is heated in the fire and removed for cooking. Place it on pads on a table, grease it, drop in a small quantity of batter, and then close it to cook. Two wafers can normally be made before it needs to be heated again.

The cast-iron cooking utensils have a tendency to rust unless they are seasoned carefully before use and kept dry when not in use. **To season a new utensil,** take corn or vegetable oil and rub it well across the entire interior and exterior of the pot before heating it over the fire. The oil will penetrate the iron to keep it from rusting. If it is used frequently to cook a variety of greasy and greaseless foods, and dried thoroughly after each use, no rust spots will appear. However, if rust spots do appear with use, they should be thoroughly scoured with any commercial scouring pad to remove the rust before reseasoning the pot. A cast-iron pot should never be left standing with wet contents.

Cast-iron trivets are indispensable in hearth cooking. They do not come into direct contact with the food, but are stands generally used to keep food warm, or melt butter with coals below. Trivets are made in a variety of ornamental shapes and sizes, and it is useful to have more than one.

While foods can be roasted on a spit by inserting prongs into each side of the meat and suspending it all from a hook over the fire, Mrs. Child recommended a tin-kitchen as far superior. Sometimes called a **reflector oven**, a **tin-kitchen** is an elaborate tin device built to stand before a hot fire, taking advantage of the heat and providing a well to catch drippings so that they can be made into gravy. The meat on the reflector-oven spit is parallel to the fire rather than perpendicular. Meat is attached firmly to the spit with skewers and twine, and is then inserted into the oven to be rotated through a complete circle during the course of the cooking time. The instructions for making the gravy as the meat cooks, as given by Mrs. Child, direct that the meat be dredged with flour before it is placed in the oven. Boiling water poured into the well is used to baste the meat during cooking. After the meat is done, the gravy is poured off, using the spout on the side, and finished to the cook's taste before serving.

After use, tin-kitchens must be scoured and kept gleaming to preserve their reflecting quality. Other **tin utensils** in nineteenth-century kitchens included tea and coffee pots, and pie plates. In general, for baking in the brick oven or in a Dutch oven, **redware** (pottery) pie plates, bowls, and baking cups are preferable to tin, for they will withstand the heat of the oven without burning the food to be cooked.

The Fire in the Hearth

Before any oven or fireplace is used, it should be checked thoroughly by a chimney sweep or other professional and, depending upon the amount of use, both chimneys should be cleaned regularly. The brick oven must have a close-fitting door with a handle. For safety, it is recommended that a fire extinguisher, in working order, and an approved fire blanket be readily accessible. Baking soda for extinguishing a grease fire and a plentiful supply of water are also sensible safety precautions.

When selecting wood for fires, hardwoods, if available, are best. They burn cleanly and produce less smoke. If the wood is damp, it will dry if it is kept indoors for a few days before it is used. If dry wood is needed in a hurry, place pieces of wood on end around the walls of the fireplace so that, as the fire burns, the wood will heat up and dry out for use.

Wood for cooking must be split. Small pieces split in half will burn more slowly with less flame. Pieces split into quarters will burn rapidly, providing the flames necessary for roasting and producing coals quickly for baking or cooking on the hearth. Kindling is needed for starting and maintaining the hearth fire and for heating the brick oven.

To build a fire on andirons, shovel old ashes and coals under them, leaving a one-inch space to allow air to circulate. Use wood shavings if available, or roll pieces of dry newspaper into tight rolls or knots and place them on top of the ashes. Lay three or four pieces of kindling on the andirons, and place three or more pieces across these. Lay two pieces of wood split in quarters across the kindling, leaving an air space between them. Light the paper, starting at the back and working toward the front. Once the kindling has caught and is burning well, place two more pieces of quarter-split wood across the two already in place.

If you do not build the fire on andirons, lay two halves of a split log directly on the fireplace floor, perpendicular to the opening of the hearth. Using the logs as andirons, prepare the fire as directed above, leaving air spaces between the logs and the back wall of the fireplace.

After the basic fire has been built and is burning well, the fire may be adjusted according to the recipe that will be prepared. For a roaring fire needed for rapid cooking for reflector ovens, and to produce coals for use with Dutch ovens, use quarter-split dry wood. Stack the logs three inches apart to allow enough air to circulate for a clear-burning fire. Crisscross the logs with kindling. A roaring fire will produce coals quickly, usually requiring one or two hours.

A moderate fire is needed for boiling and stewing. For this, use a combination of quarter- and half-split dry wood, stacking them alternately for even heat.

A slow fire is needed for slow cooking and soup stocks. Use half-split logs, set across the fire parallel to the opening of the fireplace, setting them one to two inches apart. A slow fire will build up coals gradually after two to three hours.

From experience, we know that there are four problems with hearth fires, but there are also solutions, so the cook can proceed with the recipe selected.

• A fire will not ignite properly if there is too little air. This happens when too much wood has been laid on it at the start, so that air does not circulate. When the fire is built, leave air spaces between the wood and kindling, especially when the wood is damp and will only ignite with difficulty. If the fire will not start, the only solution is to take it completely apart and rebuild it. Leave more air space and use less wood at first. Add more as the fire burns.

• If the top layer will not burn, more kindling may need to be added between layers. The kindling will flame and heat the top layer so that it will ignite.

• If the fire dies down too rapidly, the logs may be too close together. Use tongs to move the logs apart and create more air spaces. This problem may be the result of using wood that is damp or too large. If so, more kindling may be needed underneath the logs.

• After you have removed the coals to use with a Dutch oven, the fire may die down rapidly, especially if it is burning in the slow-to-moderate range. This is because the coals provide a bed of heat that will keep the logs burning. To replace the coals, place dry kindling under the logs, so that they will burn more rapidly and drop into new coals.

When cooking is is progress, the heat can be controlled by the placement of the cookware and manipulation of the fire itself. When pots are hanging from a crane, they may be raised or lowered by using additional or fewer S-hooks or trammels. If quick heat or flames are required, small pieces of split, dry wood may be added to the fire. Kettles may be moved from the end to the center of the crane, or the reverse, to be closer to or farther from the heat. Kettles on trammels may be moved away from or closer to the fire. For slow cooking, use a trivet over coals drawn out onto the hearth. For frying, melting butter, simmering, and making soft custards, the heat can be regulated by the frequency with which the coals are changed. Place a shovelful of coals on the hearth, and if your pots or skillets do not have legs, stand a wrought-iron trivet over the coals. For cooking quickly, change the coals often; for melting butter or cooking custards, change the coals less frequently.

When cooking with a reflector oven, it may be moved closer to the fire if the meat is not browning rapidly, or farther away from the flame if it is burning in spots.

When Mrs. Child wrote her book, she had one kind of oven in mind. Today we would call it a brick oven, or a bake-oven or even a beehive oven. Such an oven was constructed as part of the hearth with a large opening at about waist height. To heat this oven for use, the fire has to burn in the same space where the food to be baked will be placed. As Mrs. Child wrote in explaining the technique, "experience and observation" are two necessary ingredients for performing this operation successfully. "There is a great difference in the construction of ovens, and when an oven is extremely cold, either on account of the weather, or want of use, it must be heated more." Bake-ovens vary in construction and size. Like our predecessors, you will have to become familiar with the oven you use because "no precise rules for heating them can be given. . . . It is easy to find out how many sticks of a given size are necessary for baking articles that require a strong heat and so for those which are baked with less."

The fire in the bake-oven is laid on its floor, starting with shavings or newspaper on which kindling is arranged. Take five pieces of kindling, set them around and over the paper and light them. When the first pieces of kindling have caught, gather up a handful of kindling and feed the fire, adding another three or four pieces, and then two or three more as you see the flames receding. (Do not replace the door until the oven is loaded with food to be baked.) Kindling will burn hotter and heat the oven more quickly. After an hour, writes Mrs. Child, "stir the fire equally to all parts of the oven. This is necessary for an equal diffusion of the heat. Do it several times before the oven is cleared."

The oven must preheat for 2 hours when pies and bread are to be baked. "Let the coals remain until they are no longer red. They should not look dead, but like hot embers. When you take them out, leave in the back part a few to be put near the pans that require most heat such as beans, Indian pudding, or jars of fruit. Before putting in the things to be baked, throw in a little flour. If it browns instantly, the oven is too hot and should stand open three or four minutes. If it browns without burning in the course of half a minute, it would be safe to set in the articles immediately." Use a peel or a flat wooden implement called a shovel to remove the coals. "Some sweep the walls of the oven with a wet broom to collect ashes which might get into the food." It is not necessary to use a thermometer to test the temperature, although when learning to fire a brick oven, it may help to learn how to gauge heat. The flour test is sufficient, or put your bare arm into the oven. If you can count to ten without feeling burned, it's hot enough to use.

As a general rule, an oven will heat in two hours. Obviously, it is much easier to let a hot oven cool down than to rekindle a fire.

Now the oven is ready to use. If it is large enough to bake several items at once, the following sequence and arrangement of items may be a helpful guide.

When the oven is hot, slow-cooking foods like beans and Indian pudding should be placed near the back wall, as they will not be removed for several hours. Foods requiring high heat, including pies, bread, biscuits, and cookies, are put in to cook as soon as possible after the oven is heated. After ten minutes, biscuits and cookies are baked and may be removed. The heat is now moderate and ready for cakes to bake. Thirty minutes after the fire has been removed, cakes will be cooked. The oven heat is now low for slow-cooking foods like custards, and custard-based puddings and pies.

For the foods to cook properly, the oven should not be overcrowded. Foods to be baked are usually put into the oven in the reverse of the order in which they will be removed. In other words, beans go in first, come out last. Cookies go in last and come out first. This eliminates moving food around in the oven. When the door is open, cooler air rushes in and, as a result, breads and cakes may fall.

The cast-iron bake-kettle or Dutch oven is an alternative to the brick oven, especially if only one item is to be made. To use the bake-kettle, build a roaring fire, or obtain coals from a moderate fire that has been burning for two hours or more. Depending on the heat required, the kettle may be heated by standing it against one of the andirons. Preheat the lid by standing it against the other andiron. For hot oven temperatures, preheat kettle and lid for a half hour. For the equivalent of a moderately hot oven, preheat for 20 minutes, and for a moderate oven 10 minutes is sufficient. For custards and custard-based foods, do not preheat the kettle. If bread is to be baked, the lid may not require preheating. If the bread should rise more than a few inches, it may burn if it is too close to the hot lid. For bake-kettle cooking, the coals must have a clear, red-orange glow. If coals smoke when they are removed from the fire, they are not hot enough.

To use the bake-kettle, shovel two or three piles of coal onto the hearth, selecting a spot that will not be in the way of your movements around the hearth and oven. Set the kettle over the coals and place the food inside the kettle. Use a thick pot holder or two, and be careful not to touch the hot sides of the kettle. Set the lid on the kettle, and place two or three shovelfuls of coals on the lid. For food that will bake for a long period of time, the coals may be insulated by placing a layer of ashes over the coals on the lid and around the coals below the bake-kettle.

For pies, biscuits, and gingerbread, which require a higher baking temperature for a period of time, coals may be changed every 15 or 20 minutes. They may have to be changed after a shorter interval in cold weather, as they will cool more rapidly. Coals may be left up to 45 minutes without being changed, especially for custards and puddings which must bake slowly at a lower temperature.

While these directions are based on our experience at Old Sturbridge Village, they may not seem to be specific. Fires, fireplaces, and ovens are all subject to an individual's interpretation, as much now as in the past. Knowing one's equipment and ingredients come as the result of practice. According to Mrs. Child, "Three things must be exactly right in order to have good bread. The quantity of the yeast, the lightness or fermentation of the dough, and the heat of the oven. No precise rules can be given to ascertain these points. It requires observation, reflection and a quick, nice judgment, to decide when all are right."

Today's hearth cooks have the luxury of learning how, without having to get up in the early morning in a cold house, to prepare a big breakfast for a hungry family. However, after some practice, you will be able to rise to such an occasion. First, you will need to learn about your own fireplace and how to build and sustain a cooking fire. Once you are familiar with cooking with the cast-iron utensils as well, you will thoroughly enjoy the results. That will make up for the extra labor involved in lugging and caring for equipment that was previously unfamiliar.

It is still possible to obtain the equipment for hearth cooking without using up antique originals. The special equipment may be obtained from blacksmiths and tinsmiths who exhibit at craft fairs and who work independently. In addition, the Museum Gift Shop at Old Sturbridge Village is always a source of the tin, iron and pottery utensils which have traditionally been used. The Village reproductions have been specially selected for their authenticity.

Tin kitchens or reflector ovens are available, along with such small tin utensils as apple parers. Hand-wrought trivets, toasters, cranes and hooks are offered, many made as demonstrations by Village blacksmiths. Commercially made hanging iron pots and skillets are generally in stock at the village. New England redware in traditional forms is hand thrown, glazed, and fired as a museum demonstration. Bean pots, pie plates, mixing bowls and pitchers are among the forms available at all times. (For details on prices and shipping charges contact the Museum Gift Shop, Old Sturbridge Village, Sturbridge, MA 01566 (617) 347-3362.)

While it is charming to cook in historical costume, or even a long dress, it is more practical, at least while learning, to wear jeans and other completely washable clothes. Since you will be hovering close to the fire, you cannot avoid the smoke. In the past, a woman's day was organized so that the majority of the family's cooking was done in the morning along with preparations for the midday meal. The morning costume included a cap, because covering the hair kept it a little cleaner. Women frequently changed their clothes for the afternoon, the time for sewing and visiting.

There are many ways to enjoy hearth cooking and appreciate a taste of the past with family and friends. Cooking at least part of a meal at the hearth is entertaining for all involved once you have begun to master the techniques. Before you feel confident to cook an entire multicourse meal for company at the hearth, why not plan to make part of the meal at the fireplace — the hors d'oeuvres perhaps, or a soup or the dessert. Several of the recipes included may be made in bite-sized versions to nibble along with a drink. Roasted cheese, fish balls, small sausage patties, and potato balls lend themselves readily for appetizers, although Lydia Maria Child might be shocked at this adaptive use of the recipes of old. You might plan a simple menu, including soup and homemade bread. Cooking the soup over the fire on a winter's day keeps cook and guests together while the preparations are completed. For dessert, you might choose to use the wafer iron. You and your guests can stretch after the main course while helping to bake the thin cookies, roll them into cylinders, and fill them with whipped cream. Once you get started, you will think of other ways to make hearth cooking sociable and fun. There are some menu suggestions from nineteenth-century sources on pages 18 and 19. And remember, you don't have to cook at the hearth to recreate these meals.

Common Cooking

CDR

Roast Veal

"The shoulder of veal is the most economical for roasting or boiling. Two dinners may be made from it — the shoulder roasted and the knuckle cut off to be boiled. Six or seven pounds of veal will roast in an hour and a half."

Breast, shoulder, loin or rolled roast of veal
½ cup butter
½ cup flour
1 tsp. salt
1 tsp. crushed marjoram
   or summer savory
½ tsp. pepper

Modern Method:

1. Preheat oven to 450°.
2. Melt butter and brush over meat. Mix flour and spices. Dredge meat with seasoned flour.
3. Place prepared meat on a rack in a pan in the oven. Reduce heat immediately to 300°. Cook 30 minutes per pound.

Hearth Method:

1. Prepare reflector oven.
2. Run spit of reflector oven through center of roast. Secure with skewers.
3. Follow Step 2 in the recipe above.
4. Place spit in reflector oven. Stand reflector oven 6-10 inches from fire.
5. Turn meat at 20-minute intervals.
6. Cook 30 minutes per pound.

Servings: 4 per pound

Veal with Pork and Greens

"Veal is better for being boiled with a small piece of pork and greens."

3-4 lb. shin bone of veal
½ lb. lean pork
Water to cover meat
2-3 lb. greens, preferably fresh-picked spinach,
    lettuce, mustard, collards, etc., or herbs like lovage,
    borage, etc.*
Salt and pepper to taste

Modern Method:

1. In a heavy pot with a lid, combine meats and cover with water. Bring rapidly to a boil and simmer for 1½ hours.
2. Add chopped greens and simmer 30-40 minutes.
3. Add salt and pepper to taste before serving.

Hearth Method:

1. Use a heavy hanging kettle and combine meats with water to cover. Bring to boil as rapidly as possible over a hot fire, then let the fire die back so that the contents of the pot simmer for 1½-2 hours.
2. Follow Steps 2 and 3 in the recipe above.

Servings: 4

*If you can identify wild poke, lamb's quarter, or other wild edible greens with confidence, pick and use them. — Ed.

43

Veal Pot Roast

"Veal should boil about an hour, if a neck-piece, if the meat comes from a thicker, more solid part, it should boil longer. No directions about these things will supply the place of judgment and experience. Veal is better for being boiled with a small piece of salt pork. Veal broth is very good."

3-4 lb. rump of veal, boned and tied
½-¾ lb. pork or ham
2½ cups hot water, more for hearth cookery
1 tsp. salt, if unsalted meat is used
½ tsp. pepper, if unsalted meat is used.

Modern Method:

1. In a heavy pot with a lid, combine meats, salt, pepper, and water and cover the pot.
2. Bring rapidly to a boil, reduce heat and simmer for 2-2½ hours.
3. After an hour, turn meat and add more hot water if liquid is close to cooking away.
4. When meats are tender, transfer to a warmed platter for serving. Reserve liquid for soup or heating any leftovers.

Hearth Method:

1. Use a heavy hanging kettle, somewhat larger than the meat to be cooked. Preheat the kettle, put in meats, salt, pepper, and water so that meat is almost, but not quite, covered. Cover the pot.
2. Bring to boil as rapidly as possible over a hot fire, then let the contents of the pot simmer over the fire for about two hours.
3. Halfway through cooking period, turn the meats and check that the cooking liquid covers at least one third of

the meats. If necessary, add more hot water or broth.
4. Follow Step 4 in the recipe above.

Servings: 4

Veal Cutlets

"Fried veal is better for being dipped in white of egg, and rolled in nicely pounded crumbs of bread, before it is cooked. One egg is enough for a common dinner."

1½ lb. veal cutlets, thinly sliced
2 egg whites
¾ cup dried bread crumbs
¼ cup butter or bacon fat for frying

Modern Method:

1. Beat egg whites in one shallow bowl or pie plate, and spread bread crumbs in another bowl.
2. Dip each slice of meat in the egg white and then coat with bread crumbs.
3. Melt fat in skillet, arrange meat and fry 3-4 minutes, until browned. Turn and fry on other side.

Hearth Method:

1. Follow Steps 1 and 2 in the recipe above.
2. Follow Step 3 in the recipe above, using a hanging skillet over a moderate fire.

Servings: 4-5 depending on number and thickness of slices

Minced Meat
to Serve on Toast or as a Pie

"There is a great difference in preparing mince meat. Some make it a coarse, unsavory dish; and others make it nice and palatable. No economical house-keeper will despise it; for broken bits of meat and vegetables cannot so well be disposed of in any other way. If you wish to have it nice, mash your vegetables fine, and chop your meat very fine. Warm it with what remains of sweet gravy or roast-meat drippings, you may happen to have. Two or three apples, pared, cored, sliced and fried, to mix with it, is an improvement. Some like a little sifted sage sprinkled in.

"It is generally considered nicer to chop your meat fine, warm it in gravy, season it, and lay it upon a large slice of toasted bread to be brought upon the table without being mixed with potatoes but if you have cold vegetables, use them."

2 cups leftover roast, pot roast, etc., or 1 lb. ground beef
1 cup cooked chopped vegetables
Beef drippings or butter
2 cups apples, pared, cored, and sliced
2-3 cups gravy
½ tsp. sage
Toast points or Pie Crust (recipe on page 170)

Modern Method:

1. Chop meat if leftover roast is used. Combine meat and vegetables.
2. Melt drippings or butter in a large skillet and fry apples until soft. (If ground meat is used, remove apples from skillet, fry beef until brown, drain off grease. Put apples back into skillet.)
3. Follow Steps 1-3 in the recipe for gravy on page 60.
4. Add chopped meat, vegetables, gravy, and sage to the apples in the skillet and heat slowly.
5. Serve on toast or use as filling for meat pie. Bake meat pie 50-60 minutes at 400°.

Hearth Method:

1. Follow Steps 1-4 in the recipe above, using a large hanging skillet.
2. If a pie is desired, bake in a Dutch oven with coals above and below for 45 minutes.

Servings: 6

Pot Roast or
A La Mode Beef

"Tie up a round of beef so as to keep it in shape; make a stuffing of grated bread, suet, sweet herbs, quarter of an ounce of nutmeg, a few cloves pounded, yolk of an egg. Cut holes in the beef, and put in stuffing, leaving about half the stuffing to be made into balls. Tie the beef up in a cloth, just to cover it with water, let it boil an hour and a half; then turn it, and let it boil an hour and a half more; then turn out the liquor, and put some skewers across the bottom of the pot, and lay the beef upon it, to brown; turn it that it may brown on both sides. Put a pint of claret, and some allspice and cloves, into the liquor, and boil some balls made of the stuffing in it."

STUFFING:
2 cups grated bread crumbs, rye or whole wheat
¼ cup melted suet
1 tsp. herbs: basil, thyme, sage, or parsley
½ tsp. pepper
¼ tsp. nutmeg
¼ tsp. cloves
1 tsp. salt
1 egg yolk

POT ROAST:
5 lb. or more beef: brisket, rump, chuck, shoulder
2 cups boiling water, more for hearth cookery
Cheesecloth to wrap meat, optional
String
2 cups claret
½ tsp. allspice
½ tsp. cloves

Modern Method:

1. Combine bread crumbs, suet, herbs, salt, and egg yolk to make stuffing.
2. Cut holes into the roast to insert half of stuffing mixture. Make remaining stuffing mixture into 1-inch balls and chill.
3. Wrapping the meat is optional. (Cover meat with a clean white cheesecloth and tie securely with string.) Put meat into an oven-proof baking dish with a lid. Add boiling water. (Add additional ½ cup of water for every pound over 5 pounds.)
4. Bake in 300° oven or simmer on top of stove for 2½-3 hours, turning meat several times while cooking.
5. Pour broth into a heavy saucepan, and simmer to reduce by half. Leave meat in baking dish and return to oven to brown while gravy is made.
6. Add claret and spices to broth. Bring almost to a boil before dropping in stuffing balls. Simmer 15 minutes before serving.

Hearth Method:

1. Follow Steps 1 and 2 in the recipe above.
2. Wrapping the meat is optional. (Cover meat with a clean white cheesecloth and tie securely with string.)
3. Place meat in preheated heavy hanging kettle with lid. Just cover with hot water and bring to a rapid boil over a hot fire.
4. Maintain boiling or close to boiling temperatures for 1½ hours. Then turn meat and check cooking liquid to see that it is not boiled away and boil for 1½ hours longer.
5. Take meat out of pot, remove cheesecloth, and brown on

all sides in a hanging skillet or over hot coals.

6. While the meat is being browned, continue to cook the broth over hot fire until it is reduced by half. Add claret, allspice, and cloves. Drop stuffing balls into gravy. Simmer for 15 minutes before serving.

Servings: 2 per pound

Beef Steak

"The quicker beef-steak can be broiled the better. Seasoned after it is taken from the gridiron. The richest, tenderest and most delicate piece of beef for steak is the rump and the last cut of the sirloin."

Sirloin, T-bone, or porterhouse steak, 2 in. thick

Modern Method:

1. Preheat broiler.
2. Let steak warm to room temperature before broiling.
3. Broil 5-7 minutes on first side; turn and broil 4-5 minutes.

Hearth Method:

1. Preheat gridiron over coals.
2. Put steak on gridiron and put fresh coals below.
3. Broil for 5-7 minutes.
4. Turn meat and place gridiron over fresh coals.
5. Broil 5 minutes.

Servings: 2-3 per pound

Roast Beef

"A quarter of an hour to each pound of beef is considered a good rule for roasting; but this is too much when the bone is large and the meat thin. Six pounds of the rump should roast six quarters of an hour, but bony pieces less. It should be done before a quick fire. The richest, tenderest and most delicate piece of beef for roasting is the rump and the last cut of the sirloin. If economy be consulted instead of luxury, the round will be bought in preference to the rump."

Rib, sirloin or other beef suitable for oven roasting
Gravy, optional

Modern Method:

1. Preheat the oven to 500°.
2. If gravy is desired, follow Steps 1-3 in the recipe on page 60.
3. Place the roast, fat side up, on a rack in a pan, and reduce heat to 350°.
4. For medium to medium rare, cook 18-20 minutes per pound. If cooking a rolled roast, allow 25 minutes per pound.

Hearth Method:

1. Prepare reflector oven.
2. Run spit through meat lengthwise, and secure with skewers.
3. If gravy is desired, follow Steps 1-3 in the recipe on page 60.
4. Place reflector oven 6-10 inches from fire.
5. Allow 20-25 minutes per pound, turning spit every 20 minutes.

Servings: 3-4 per pound if boneless cut of beef is used
1-2 per pound if meat has bone

Beef Soup

"Beef soup should be stewed four hours over a slow fire. Just water enough to keep the meat covered. If you have any bones left of roast meat, &c. it is a good plan to boil them with the meat, and take them out half an hour before the soup is done. A pint of flour and water, with salt, pepper, twelve or sixteen onions, should be put in twenty minutes before the soup is done. Be careful and do not throw in salt and pepper too plentifully; it is easy to add to it, and not easy to diminish. A lemon, cut up and put in half an hour before it is done, adds to the flavor. If you have tomato catsup in the house, a cupful will make soup rich. Some people put in crackers, some thin slices of crust, made nearly as short as common shortcake; and some stir up two or three eggs with milk and flour, and drop it in with a spoon."

5-6 lb. beef bones — for richer flavor use a combination of bones with meat; shank, short ribs or bones from which a roast has been carved
4 qt. water
6-8 medium to large onions
1 cup flour
2 cups water
1 tsp. salt
1 tsp. pepper
¾ cup catsup, optional (recipe on page 218)
1 sliced lemon, optional

DUMPLINGS:
Crackers or cubed crusts or toasted bread
1 egg
¼ cup milk
1 cup flour

Modern Method:

1. Place the beef bones in a large stockpot and cover with water. Simmer slowly, uncovered, for 2-3 hours.
2. Remove meat from bones and cut it up. Discard bones.
3. Put meat and broth back into saucepan and return to heat. There will be about 2 quarts of broth. Add onions, whole or chopped. To thicken, make a paste of the flour and water and stir gradually into soup. Simmer 15 minutes. Season with salt and pepper, add catsup or lemon, or make dumplings, if desired.
4. To make dumplings, beat together egg and milk. Stir in flour until blended. Drop batter by spoonfuls into pot of soup to simmer during last half hour of cooking.
5. Serve soup with crackers or cubed crusts or toasted bread.

Hearth Method:

1. Place the beef bones in a large hanging kettle, cover with water. Bring to boil over a hot fire, then remove from hottest fire, or let it die back, while contents of pot simmer for 3½ hours.
2. Follow Steps 2 and 3 in the recipe above, over hot fire.
3. Follow Steps 4 and 5 in the recipe above.

Servings: 10-12

Corned Beef

"When you merely want to corn meat, you have nothing to do but to rub in salt plentifully and let it set in the cellar a day or two. The navel end of the brisket is one of the best pieces for corning.

"A six pound piece of corned beef should boil three full hours. Put it in to boil when the water is cold. If you boil it in a small pot, it is well to change the water, when it has boiled an hour and a half; the fresh water should boil before the half-cooked meat is put in again."

2 cups salt
1 gal. hot water
3-6 lb. brisket of beef
Cold water to cover meat

Modern Method:

1. To corn the beef, make up a brine solution by dissolving 1½ cups of salt in a gallon of hot water in a large enamelled, glass, or stoneware pot. Cool.
2. Rub remaining ½ cup salt into meat. Place the meat in the cooled brine solution, covering with a weight to keep the meat submerged in the brine. Refrigerate or set in a cool place for 48 hours.
3. To cook, rinse meat and place in a large cooking pot with a lid. Cover with water and bring to a boil.
4. Simmer, covered, 3-4 hours, until tender. Add more boiling water, if necessary.

Hearth Method:

1. Follow Steps 1 and 2 in the recipe above.
2. Follow Step 3 in the recipe above, using a large hanging pot.
3. Simmer for about 1½-2 hours, adding more boiling water

for the last 1½ hours of cooking. Make sure that the fire is hot enough for the water in the pot to simmer for the entire cooking period.

Servings: 2-3 per pound

Pork Sausage

"Three teaspoons of powdered sage, one and a half of salt and one of pepper, to a pound of meat, is good seasoning for sausages."

1 lb. salted casings (if link sausages are desired)
1 lb. lean ground or finely chopped pork
3 tsp. powdered sage
1½ tsp. salt
1 tsp. pepper

Modern Method and Hearth Method

1. Soak casings in cold water, according to package directions. Drain and place on towels to dry off, but keep moist for use.
2. Blend pork and seasonings thoroughly.
3. Stuff casings using a manual sausage stuffer or electric grinder attachment. If a manual stuffer is used, warm meat slightly before stuffing the casings. Or shape seasoned meat into patties.
4. Fry over low heat until well cooked in a skillet on a stove or over a hot fire at the hearth.

Servings: 4

Pork Roast

"Fresh pork should be cooked more than any other meat. A thick shoulder piece should be roasted full two hours and a half; and other pieces less in proportion."

Loin rib or shoulder of pork
1 cup flour
1 tsp. salt
1 tsp. sage
½ tsp. pepper
1 cup water

Modern Method:

1. Preheat oven to 450°.
2. If gravy is desired, mix the flour, salt, sage, and pepper and dredge seasoned flour over meat and place on rack in a pan. Pour water into pan. Reduce oven heat immediately to 350°.
3. Cook rolled or boneless roast 40 minutes per pound. Cook a loin or rib roast with bones in for 30-35 minutes per pound.

Hearth Method:

1. Prepare reflector oven.
2. Run spit through center of roast; secure with skewers. If gravy is desired, mix the flour, salt, sage, and pepper, and dredge seasoned flour over meat. Pour water into base of reflector oven, and set in front of fire 6-10 inches away from it.
3. Follow Step 3 in the recipe above, turning the spit at 20-minute intervals.

Servings: 2-3 per pound

Salt Pork and Apples

"Fried salt pork and apples is a favorite dish in the country, but it is seldom seen in the city. After the pork is fried, some of the fat should be taken out, lest the apples should be oily. Acid apples should be chosen, because they cook more easily; they should be cut in slices across the whole apple, about twice or three times as thick as a new dollar. Fried until tender and brown on both sides laid around the pork. If you have cold potatoes, slice them and brown them in the same way."

1-2 thick slices salt pork
3 medium apples
2-3 cooked potatoes
1 lb. pork, cut up, or 4-6 pork chops

Modern Method:

1. Cut salt pork into small thin pieces and render the fat.
2. Core and slice the apples, and slice the potatoes.
3. Cook cut-up pork or chops in the pan in which the salt pork has been rendered. Fry 20-25 minutes.
4. If skillet is large enough, push meat to one side; otherwise transfer to serving platter and keep warm. Check to see if there is sufficient fat for frying. If not, render a second slice of salt pork to fry apples and potatoes until browned.
5. To serve, arrange fried apples and potatoes around meat on serving platter.

Hearth Method:

1. Follow Steps 1 and 2 in the recipe above.
2. Render salt pork in a hanging skillet. Add cut-up pork or chops and fry 20-25 minutes.
3. Follow Steps 4 and 5 in the recipe above.

Servings: 4

Beans

"Baked beans are a very simple dish, yet few cook them well. They should be put in cold water, and hung over the fire, the night before they are baked. In the morning, they should be put in a colander, and rinsed two or three times; then again placed in a kettle, with the pork you intend to bake, covered with water, and kept scalding hot, an hour or more. A pound of pork is quite enough for a quart of beans, and that is a large dinner for a common family. The rind of the pork should be slashed. Pieces of pork alternately fat and lean, are the most suitable; the cheeks are the best. A little pepper sprinkled among the beans, when they are placed in the bean-pot, will render them less unhealthy. They should be just covered with water, when put into the oven; and the pork should be sunk a little below the surface of the beans. Bake three or four hours."

[This recipe is intended to make a meal of pork and beans. Mrs. Child is describing "pieces of pork" which are both "fat and lean," rather than fatty chunks of salt pork. Furthermore, the use of a pound of salt pork of the kind available at supermarkets today would result in a greasy and salty pot of pork and beans. Either reduce the quantity of pork, if intended as a side dish, or use a combination of fresh and salt pork for a meal.

In her 1845 cookbook, Mrs. Esther A. Howland recommended that the cook "dissolve a lump of saleratus as big as a walnut with your beans before making and you will find them greatly improved." Saleratus is baking soda. — *Ed.]*

1 lb. dried beans
Water to cover beans
¾ lb. boneless pork, cubed
½ lb. salt pork, cut in thin slices
1 tsp. pepper

Modern Method:

1. Soak beans in water at room temperature overnight.
2. Drain, reserving water. Rinse beans thoroughly.
3. Layer beans and pork in a heavy saucepan. Add reserved water. Bring to boil and simmer for 1 hour.
4. To bake, transfer beans, pork, and water into a bean pot or other oven-proof casserole with a lid. Season with pepper. There should be enough liquid to just cover beans. Add hot water, if necessary.
5. Bake 4-6 hours. If a crock pot or slow cooker is used, cook beans and pork on high heat for an hour or more. Turn heat to low and cook 10-12 hours or overnight.

Hearth Method:

1. Soak beans in water overnight. If fireplace has been used, hang beans in a pot of water over remaining coals, otherwise soak in a bowl at room temperature.
2. Follow Step 2 in the recipe above.
3. Layer beans and pork in a hanging kettle. Add reserved water. Bring to a boil over a hot fire and cook for 1 hour.
4. To bake, transfer beans, pork, and water to a bean pot. Season with pepper.
5. Place bean pot toward the back of a preheated brick oven, where it will not be disturbed as other foods are baked. Leave 4-6 hours or overnight. As the oven cools, the beans will cook.

Yield: 8 cups or more depending on variety of beans used

Gravy

"Most people put a half a pint of flour and water into their tin-kitchen when they set meat down to roast. This does very well; but gravy is better flavored, and looks darker, to shake flour and salt upon the meat; let it brown thoroughly, put flour and salt on again, and then baste the meat with about half a pint of hot water (or more, according to the gravy you want). When the meat is about done, pour these drippings into a skillet, and let it boil, and be well stirred, after the flour is in. If you fear it will be too greasy, take off a cupful of the fat before you boil. The fat of beef, pork, turkeys and geese is as good for shortening as lard. Salt gravy to your taste. If you are very particular about dark gravies, keep your dredging-box full of scorched flour for that purpose."

1 cup flour
1 cup water
2-3 tsp. flour to finish gravy preparation
Salt and pepper to taste

Modern Method:

1. Sprinkle flour and water into baking pan beneath the meat, so that drippings will blend into gravy as the meat cooks.
2. After cooking period for meat is complete, allow meat to rest for 15 minutes in the roasting pan, while additional juices collect.
3. Remove meat to warmed platter for carving or serving. Look at the gravy mixture. If it seems too greasy, remove some fat, or if too thin, add more flour a teaspoonful at a time. Heat to boiling to cook the flour thoroughly before serving. Add salt and pepper to taste.

Hearth Method:

1. Sprinkle flour and water in the base of reflector oven, so

that drippings will blend into gravy as the meat cooks.
2. After cooked meat is removed from skewer in reflector oven, pour off or spoon out the liquids that have accumulated into a hanging skillet.
3. If the gravy seems too greasy, remove some fat, or if too thin, add more flour a teaspoonful at a time. Heat to boiling to cook the flour before serving. Add salt and pepper to taste.

Yield: 1-2 cups

Scorched or Browned Flour

1 cup flour

Modern Method:

1. Place flour in a heavy skillet over low heat. Stir until golden brown, 15-20 minutes.

Hearth Method:

1. Follow Step 1 in the recipe above, using a spider over the coals.

Yield: 1-2 cups

"Better-Flavored Gravy"

1 cup flour, plain or scorched
2 tsp. salt
1 cup hot water, or more, if more gravy is desired

Modern Method:

1. Roll meat in mixture of flour and salt before roasting.
2. Halfway through cooking time, dredge remaining flour and salt over meat. Pour 1 cup hot water over meat and return to oven.
3. Follow Steps 2 and 3 of the recipe for gravy above.

Hearth Method:

1. Sift ½ cup of flour and 1 teaspoon of salt over skewered meat before the spit is inserted into the reflector oven.
2. After an hour, before turning the spit again, shake remaining flour over meat. Pour water over the floured meat.
3. Follow Steps 2 and 3 of the recipe for gravy above.

Yield: 1-2 cups

"Progressive Agriculture — May Washington's example as a Farmer guide us in the principles of husbandry."

— Source Unknown

Roast Lamb or Mutton

"Six or seven pounds of mutton will roast in an hour and a half. Lamb one hour. The breast or shoulder of mutton are both nice for roasting, boiling or broth. The loin of lamb is suitable for roasting."

5 lb. leg or shoulder of lamb or mutton
1 tsp. crushed sage or summer savory
Gravy, optional

Modern Method:

1. Preheat oven to 450°
2. To prepare meat for cooking remove the fell, the paper-like outside covering. Using a pointed knife, insert pinches of crushed herbs under the skin.
3. If gravy is desired, follow Steps 1-3 in the recipe for gravy on page 60.
4. Place meat, fat side up, on a pan with a rack and put in the oven. Reduce the heat immediately to 350° and roast 25 minutes per pound.

Hearth Method:

1. Prepare reflector oven.
2. Follow steps 2 and 3 in the recipe above.
3. Insert spit of reflector oven through meat and secure with skewers. Put reflector oven in front of the fire.
4. Cook 25 minutes to the pound, rotating spit every 20 minutes.

Servings: 6-7

Braised Lamb or Mutton

"Breast or shoulder of mutton is nice for boiling. Either fore-quarter or hind quarter of lamb is good for boiling. The leg is more suitable for boiling than for anything else, the shoulder and breast are peculiarly suitable for broth.

"Fresh meat should never be put in to cook till the water boils; and it should be boiled in as little water as possible; otherwise the flavor is injured. Mutton enough for a family of five or six should boil in an hour and a half. A leg of lamb should boil an hour, or a little more than hour, perhaps. Put a little thickening into boiling water; strain it nicely; and put sweet butter in for sauce."

5 lb. leg or shoulder of lamb or mutton
4 cups water, 6 cups or more for hearth cookery
½ cup flour
1 cup boiling water
¼ cup butter
Salt and pepper to taste

Modern Method:

1. Remove the fell, the paperlike outer covering on the meat.
2. Bring water to a boil in a cooking pot large enough for the piece of meat. Put the meat in when the water boils, and cover the pot. Reduce the heat and simmer 30 minutes per pound. Add more boiling water, if necessary.
3. Remove meat to a heated platter and keep it warm while the gravy is made. Make a paste with ½ cup flour and boiling water, and blend it slowly into cooking liquid, stirring until it thickens. Add butter and stir until it melts. Season with salt and pepper to taste.

Hearth Method:

1. Follow Step 1 in the recipe above.
2. Boil water in a hanging pot and place meat in the pot. The meat should not be submerged, but add more water to maintain moisture for cooking. Simmer covered, for 30 minutes per pound.
3. Follow Step 3 in the recipe above.

Servings: 5-6

At one o'clock came dinner; always a large joint roast or boiled, with plenty of vegetables and few condiments, — for she thought them unwholesome, good bread and butter and a plain pudding or pie.

If it was to be a tea-party, she had only to order an abundant supply of tea and coffee, with thin slices of bread and butter doubled, sponge cake made by the daughters before breakfast and thin slices of cold tongue or ham; if an evening party, the lemonade and cake and wine in summer, and the nuts and raisins and fine apples in winter, furnished the simple but sufficient entertainment.

— Susan I. Lesley, *Recollections of My Mother*, Boston, 1899

Turkey

"A good sized turkey [about 8 lb. back then — Ed.] should be roasted two hours and a half, or three hours; very slowly at first. If you wish to make plain stuffing, pound a cracker, or crumble some bread very fine, chop some raw salt pork very fine, sift some sage, (and summer savory, or sweet marjoram, if you have them in the house, and fancy them,) and mould them all together, seasoned with a little pepper. An egg worked in makes the stuffing cut better; but it is not worth while when eggs are dear. About the same length of time is required for boiling and roasting."

STUFFING:
6 common crackers or ½ loaf of bread
½ cup chopped pork or sausage meat
1 tsp. sage
½ tsp. summer savory or sweet marjoram, optional
½ tsp. pepper
1 egg

GRAVY:
1 cup water
1 cup flour
Salt and pepper to taste

Modern Method:

1. Preheat oven to 450°.
2. Pound crackers or grate bread into soft crumbs.
3. Mix remaining ingredients with cracker or bread crumbs.
4. Stuff the bird and secure the cavity with poultry lacers or sew it together.
5. If gravy is desired, follow steps 1-3 in the recipe on page 60.
6. Put bird on a rack in a pan and into the oven. Reduce heat to 350°. Roast 25 minutes per pound.

Hearth Method:

1. Prepare fire and reflector oven.
2. Follow Steps 2-4 in the recipe above.
3. Push spit through the bird parallel to the backbone. (The number of skewers needed will depend on the size of the bird.) Push skewers at a right angle to spit, securing it through the holes in the spit. Using string, tie legs and wings securely to the bird. Dredge bird with flour and salt mixture.
4. Insert spit in tin kitchen, place it 10-12 inches from the fire. Rotate spit every 15 minutes. Dredge with remainder of flour and pour hot water over bird after 1.hour and move oven toward fire, so that it is 6-8 inches away from heat. Roast about 25 minutes per pound. When bird is done, remove from spit to serve.
5. If gravy is desired, follow Steps 2 and 3 of the recipe on page 60.

Servings: 1 serving per pound

Broiled Chicken

"In broiling chickens, it is difficult to do the inside of the thickest pieces without scorching the outside. It is a good plan to parboil them about 10 minutes in a spider or skillet, covered close to keep the steam in, then put them upon the gridiron, broil and butter. It is a good plan to cover them with a plate, while on the gridiron. They may be basted with a very little of the water in which they were parboiled; and if you have company who like melted butter to pour upon the chicken, the remainder of the liquor will be good used for that purpose."

Broiling chicken 2-3 lb., cut up
1 cup water
¼ cup butter, optional

Modern Method:

1. Preheat broiler or barbecue grill.
2. Parboil chicken in water in a tightly covered pan for 10 minutes.
3. Put chicken, skin side down, on preheated broiling pan. Reserve broth.
4. Broil 10 minutes, turn and baste with reserved broth. Broil 8-10 minutes more, or until browned.
5. Serve with melted butter, if desired

Hearth Method:

1. Follow Step 2 in the recipe above.
2. Draw coals out onto hearth, and preheat gridiron. Arrange chicken parts and cover with a plate. Reserve broth. Broil 25 minutes.
3. Turn chicken, draw out more coals, put gridiron over fresh coals, and baste with reserved broth. Cover and broil 20 minutes.

4. Melt butter or heat remaining broth in front of fire.
5. Place chicken on a warmed serving platter. Pass melted butter or broth, if desired.

Servings: 1 per ¾ lb.

Iron Pot

Roast Chicken with Stuffing

"An hour is enough for common sized chickens to roast. A smart fire is better than a slow one; but they must be tended closely. Slices of bread, buttered, salted and peppered, put into the stomach (not the crop) are excellent."

STUFFING:
4-5 slices of bread: rye, whole wheat, corn, etc.
4 tbl. butter
Salt and pepper to taste

4-5 lb. roasting chicken

GRAVY:
1 cup water
1 cup flour
Salt and pepper to taste

Modern Method:

1. Preheat oven to 450°.
2. Slice bread, and butter and season to taste. Fill cavity loosely and secure the opening with poultry lacers for a large bird, or by sewing it closed for a smaller one.
3. For gravy, sift flour and salt together and dredge half of mixture over poultry.
4. Place on rack in a pan. Reduce heat to 350°. Roast 20 minutes per pound.
5. After 1 hour shake remaining flour and salt over bird and pour 1 cup boiling water over it.
6. When chicken is cooked, finish gravy by skimming off extra fat or adding flour, if needed. Cook to blend, correct seasoning and serve hot.

Hearth Method:

1. Prepare reflector oven.
2. Slice bread, and butter and season to taste. Fill cavity loosely, reserving prepared heel or crust of bread for last to cover opening of cavity.
3. For gravy, place water in base of reflector oven and dredge the bird with half of the seasoned flour.
4. Run spit through prepared bird, securing legs and wings with string.
5. Insert spit in reflector oven and place 6-10 inches from fire. Rotate spit every 20 minutes.
6. For gravy, halfway through cooking period, dredge remaining seasoned flour over bird and baste with hot water.
7. When chicken is cooked, remove from spit. Ladle or pour gravy mixture into a hanging skillet. Remove fat or add flour, as required. Cook to blend, correct seasoning and serve hot.

Servings: 1 per ¾ pound

Stewed Chicken,
with Broth to Serve Separately

"Chickens should boil about an hour. If old, they should boil longer. In as little water as will cook them. Chicken broth made like mutton broth.

"If your family like broth, throw in some clean rice when you put in the meat. The rice should be in proportion to the quantity of broth you mean to make. A large tablespoonful is enough for three pints of water. Seasoned with a very little pepper and salt. Summer savory, or sage, rubbed through a sieve, thrown in."

4-5 lb. whole chicken, washed
2 cups water, more for hearth cookery
2-4 tbl. rice
1 tsp. salt
½ tsp. pepper
1 tsp. sifted summer savory or sage

Herb and Spice Box

Modern Method:

1. Place chicken in a saucepan with 2 cups water. Add rice and seasonings if flavored broth or chicken soup is desired.
2. Bring to a boil, skim the pot, cover and simmer for 1¼ hours.
3. When cooked, remove chicken from broth. The chicken may be served hot or cooled for use in chicken salad.* Chicken broth with rice should be refrigerated until ready to use.

Hearth Method:

1. Place whole chicken in a hanging kettle. Add cold water until chicken is almost covered. Add rice and seasonings, if broth or soup is desired.
2. Bring to a boil over hot fire, pull away from heat to skim. Cover pot and simmer for 1½ hours.
3. Follow Step 3 in recipe above.

Servings: 5-6

*A serving suggestion from the nineteenth century: Cut a small head of cabbage into wedges and add to pot for the last ½ hour of cooking. In the past, this was a frequent combination, served even at Thanksgiving. — *Ed.*

Chicken Fricassee, Brown

"Singe the chickens; cut them in pieces; pepper, salt, and flour them; fry them in fresh butter, till they are very brown: take the chickens out, and make a good gravy, into which put sweet herbs (marjoram or sage) according to your taste; if necessary, add pepper and salt; butter and flour must be used in making the gravy, in such quantities as to suit yourself for thickness and richness. After this is all prepared, the chicken must be stewed in it, for half an hour, closely covered. A pint of gravy is about enough for two chickens; I should think a piece of butter about as big as a walnut, and a table-spoonful of flour, would be enough for the gravy. The herbs should, of course, be pounded and sifted. Some, who love onions, slice two or three, and brown them with the chicken. Some slice a half lemon, and stew with the chicken. Some add tomatoes catsup."

3-4 lb. chicken, cut up, or parts
2-3 onions
¾ cup whole wheat flour
1 tsp. salt
1 tsp. pepper
¼-½ cup butter
2 cups boiling water
½ lemon, optional
½ cup catsup, optional (recipe on page 218)
1 tbl. sage or marjoram

Modern Method:

1. Slice onions and lemon, and set aside.
2. Rinse chicken.
3. Mix flour, salt, and pepper. Dredge chicken with seasoned flour.
4. Melt butter in a large skillet or flame-proof casserole with a cover. Fry chicken pieces for five minutes on each side,

or until browned. Add more butter, if needed. Remove chicken. Fry onions and push aside.

5. There should be about 2 tablespoons or more of butter left in the skillet. Add an equal amount of the remaining seasoned flour. Stir to make a paste, cook briefly and then add boiling water, stirring until gravy thickens.

6. Season with herbs and lemon or catsup, if desired. Add chicken. Cover closely and simmer for about ½ hour. If there is too much fat, skim it off before serving.

Hearth Method:

1. Follow Steps 1-3 in the recipe above.

2. Melt butter in a hanging pot or large hanging skillet. Fry chicken pieces for five minutes on each side or until browned. Add more butter, if needed. Remove chicken. Fry onions.

3. Push onions to one side and allow remaining butter to drain down to one edge of skillet. There should be 2 tablespoons or more butter remaining in skillet. Add an equal amount of the remaining seasoned flour. Stir to make a paste, push pot back over fire, and cook briefly. Carefully add boiling water away from the fire, stirring until gravy thickens.

4. Follow Step 6 in the recipe above.

Servings: 1 per ¾ pound

Chicken Fricassee, White

"The chickens are cut to pieces, and covered with warm water, to draw out the blood. Then put into a stew-pan, with three quarters of a pint of water, or veal broth, salt, pepper, flour, butter, mace, sweet herbs pounded and sifted; boil it half an hour. If it is too fat, skim it a little. Just before it is done, mix the yolk of two eggs with a gill of cream, grate in a little nutmeg, stir it up till it is thick and smooth, squeeze in half a lemon. If you like onions, stew some slices with the other ingredients."

3-lb. whole chicken, or parts
2 tbl. butter
2 tbl. flour
1½ cups hot water or broth
1 tsp. salt
½ tsp. pepper
½ tsp. mace
1 tbl. sage or marjoram
2 egg yolks
¼ cup cream
¼ tsp. nutmeg
Juice of ½ lemon
Large onion, optional

Modern Method:

1. Cut chicken into small pieces (only soak in warm water if freshly killed). If desired, cut onion into thin slices.
2. In a large skillet or flame-proof casserole melt butter and add flour to make a paste. Stir in hot water or broth, and continue stirring until it thickens. Add chicken, onion if desired, salt, pepper, mace, and sage or marjoram. Cook for 30-45 minutes in all. Before serving skim fat if necessary.
3. Just before serving, beat two egg yolks, add cream and

76

nutmeg. Pour slowly into chicken and sauce. Squeeze lemon over all and heat through, but do not boil.

Hearth Method:

1. Follow Steps 1 and 2 in the recipe above, using a hanging skillet.
2. Follow Step 3 in the recipe above, removing skillet from fire to add ingredients.

Servings: 1 per ¾ pound

Beanpot

To Curry Fowl

"Fry out two or three slices of salt pork; cut the chicken in pieces, and lay it in the stew-pan with one sliced onion; when the fowl is tender, take it out, and put in thickening into the liquor, one spoonful of flour, and one spoonful of curry-powder, well stirred up in water. Then lay the chicken in again, and let it boil up a few minutes. A half a pint of liquor is enough for one chicken. About half an hour's stewing is necessary. The juice of half a lemon improves it; and some like a spoonful of tomatoes catsup."

3 lb. chicken, or parts
3 slices salt pork, ¼-in. thick
1 medium onion
2 cups water, more for hearth cookery
2 tbl. flour
2 tbl. curry powder
½ cup water
Juice of ½ lemon, optional
1 tbl. catsup, optional (recipe on page 218)

Modern Method:

1. Wash chicken and cut into pieces; slice the onion and chop the pork.
2. Fry salt pork in a deep skillet or flame-proof casserole until crisp. Remove crisped pork.
3. Saute onion in hot fat and push aside. Brown chicken on both sides.
4. Cover with water and simmer ½ hour until chicken is tender. Remove chicken.
5. Mix flour, curry powder, and water. Stir into cooking juices and cook 5 minutes or until thickened. Add lemon and/or catsup, if desired.
6. Put the chicken back into the skillet and reheat before serving.

Hearth Method:

1. Follow Step 1 in the recipe above.
2. In a hanging skillet, fry salt pork until crisp. Pull from direct heat and remove crisped pork.
3. Follow Step 3 in the recipe above.
4. Add 2 cups water, or a little more to cover the chicken. Bring to a boil and simmer for ½ hour until chicken is tender. Pull off heat and remove chicken.
5. Mix flour, curry powder, and water. Stir into cooking juices and return to fire. Cook 5 minutes or until thickened.
6. Follow Step 6 in recipe above.

Servings: 1 per ¾ pound

"May Fortune be always an attendant on Virtue."
"May mirth and good fellowship be always in fashion."
"Success to the fair sex in all their undertakings."
"May help bind him whom honor can't."
"May we never taste the Apples of Affliction."

— Arithmetic Schoolbook, Old Sturbridge Village manuscript
(c. 1792)

Chicken Broth
(A Hearty Meal)

*"Cut a chicken in quarters; put it into three or four quarts of water;
put in a cup of rice while the water is cold; season it with pepper
and salt; some use nutmeg. Let it stew gently, until the chicken
falls apart. A little parsley, shred fine, is an improvement. Some
slice up a small onion and stew with it. A few pieces of cracker
may be thrown in if you like."*

Small chicken, under 3 lbs., washed
3-4 qt. water
¾-1 cup rice
1 tsp. salt
1 tsp. pepper
⅛ tsp. nutmeg
1 small whole onion
¼ cup fresh parsley, chopped
½ cup crumbled crackers

Modern Method:

1. Cut chicken into quarters, put in saucepan and add water.
2. Add rice, salt, pepper, nutmeg, and onion.
3. Bring to a boil, skim and simmer gently for about 3 hours
   or until chicken falls apart.
4. Before serving, remove bones and skim off extra fat. Add
   parsley and crumbled crackers, heat and serve.

Hearth Method:

1. Follow Steps 1 and 2 in the recipe above, using a hanging
   kettle.
2. Bring to a boil over a moderate fire, pull away from heat to
   skim. Return to heat to simmer gently for 3 hours or until

chicken falls apart.
3. Follow Step 4 in the recipe above.

Servings: 4 servings

Ham

"To boil hams, they should be put on in cold water, the chill taken off and simmered for four to five hours, taking care not to allow them to boil."

1 smoked ham
Water to cover ham

Modern Method:

1. Select a pot large enough to hold ham and plenty of cold water.
2. Bring to a boil, reduce heat and simmer uncovered 20-30 minutes per pound.

Hearth Method:

1. Use a large hanging pot. Cover ham with cold water and place over a hot fire until it comes to a simmer.
2. Maintain simmer, allowing 20-30 minutes per pound.

Servings: 2-3 per pound

Meat Pie

"A nice way of serving up cold chicken, or pieces of cold fresh meat, is to make them into a meat pie. The gizzards, livers, and necks of poultry, parboiled, are good for the same purpose. If you wish to bake your meat pie, line a deep earthen or tin pan with paste made of flour, cold water, and lard; use but little lard, for the fat of the meat will shorten the crust. Lay in your bits of meat, or chicken, with two or three slices of salt pork; place a few thin slices of your paste here and there; drop in an egg or two if you have plenty. Fill the pan with flour and water, seasoned with a little pepper and salt. If the meat be very lean, put in a piece of butter, or such sweet gravies as you may happen to have. Cover the top with crust, and put it in the oven, or bake-kettle, to cook half an hour, or an hour, according to the size of the pie. Some people think this the nicest way of cooking fresh chickens. When thus cooked, they should be parboiled before they are put into the pan, and the water they are boiled in should be added. A chicken pie needs to be cooked an hour and a half, if parboiled; two hours if not."

PIE-CRUST FOR 9-IN. PIE:
2 cups flour
⅓ cup lard or other shortening
¼ cup water

FILLING:
2-3 cups cooked chicken, giblets, parboiled cut-up whole
    chicken, or any other cooked, chopped meat
¼ cup chopped salt pork
2 eggs
1 cup meat gravy (see recipe on page 60) or 1 cup chicken
    broth and ¼ cup flour
Salt and pepper to taste

Modern Method:

1. Make pie crust. Measure flour into bowl. Cut lard or shortening into flour, working until well blended. Make a depression in the center of this mixture, pour in water and mix rapidly by hand to blend. Divide this dough to make two 9-in. crusts. Roll out one ball of dough to line pie plate with crust. Trim strips of dough from around edges and reserve.
2. Layer chopped meat and pork in pie crust. Put trimmed scraps of pie crust in around the edges. If broth is used instead of gravy, sprinkle ¼ cup flour over top of filling.
3. Beat eggs with a fork, and combine with gravy or broth. Add salt and pepper to taste. Pour mixture over filling.
4. Cover pie with remaining crust; prick with a fork.
5. Bake 40 minutes at 375° or until top is browned.

Hearth Method:

1. Preheat bake-oven or prepare coals if Dutch oven is used.
2. Follow steps 1-4 in the recipe above.
3. Bake 1 hour, or a little less in Dutch oven.

Servings: 6

Fried Fish

"Cod has white stripes, and a haddock black stripes; they may be known apart by this. Haddock is the best for frying and cod is the best for boiling, or for a chowder. A thin tail is a sign of a poor fish; always choose a thick fish.

"When you are buying a mackerel, pinch the belly to ascertain whether it is good. If it gives under your finger, like a bladder half filled with wind, the fish is poor; if it feels hard like butter, the fish is good. It is cheaper to buy one large mackerel for ninepence, than two for four pence half-penny each.

"Fish should not be put in to fry until the fat is boiling hot; it is very necessary to observe this. It should be dipped in Indian meal before it is put in; and the skinny side uppermost, when first put in to prevent its breaking. It relishes better to be fried after salt pork, than to be fried in lard alone."

Fresh or frozen fish, whole or filleted
2-4 oz. salt pork, bacon drippings, or fat reserved from another fish fry
White cornmeal

Modern Method:

1. Cut salt pork into small thick strips and render fat for frying the fish.
2. Wash the fish and coat with cornmeal.
3. Place prepared fish into sizzling fat. Cook the fish 3-5 minutes on each side, turning once.

Hearth Method:

1. Follow Steps 1 and 2 in the recipe above, using either a hanging skillet or spider over coals.
2. Fish will cook more rapidly in a hanging skillet over a hot

flame. If using a spider on a trivet, preheat spider over coals, and use fresh coals when fish is added and turned. Cook 8-10 minutes on each side.

Servings: 1 per ¾ pound of whole fish
*   1 per ⅓ pound of fillet*

Earthenware Jars

Fish Gravy

"Fish gravy is very much improved by taking out some of the fat after the fish is fried, and putting in a little butter. The fat thus taken out will do to fry fish again; but it will not do for any kind of shortening. Shake in a little flour into the hot fat, and pour in a little boiling water; stir it up well, as it boils, a minute or so. Some people put in vinegar; but this is easily added by those who like it."

1 tbl. butter
1 tbl. fat in which fish was fried
2 tbl. flour
1 cup boiling water
2 tbl. vinegar or dry white wine, optional (see recipes for herb vinegars page 129)

Modern Method and Hearth Method:

1. Melt butter and remaining fat in skillet; add flour.
2. Add boiling water gradually, stirring until gravy thickens and is smooth. Add vinegar or wine and mix well.

Yield: 1 1/8 cups

Breakfast between 4 and 5, newly caught trout, salmon, ham, boiled eggs and other niceties — truly excellent.

— Nathaniel Hawthorne, *The American Notebooks* (New Haven, 1932), July 27, 1838

Broiled Fish

"The fire for broiling fish must be very clear and the gridiron perfectly clean, which when hot, should be rubbed with a bit of suet. The fish, while broiling, must be often turned. Garnish with slices of lemon, finely scraped horseradish, fried oysters, smelts, whitings or strips of soles."

Fresh fish, whole, trimmed, or fish steak
Suet
Lemon slices, grated horseradish, fried oysters, smelts, or other small fish or fish slices for garnish

Modern Method:

1. Preheat broiler.
2. Grease broiling pan with suet before putting on the fish, skin side down. Flat or thin fish should broil 2 inches from the heat for 3-4 minutes. They will not need to be turned. Thick and large pieces of fish should broil 6 inches from the heat for 5-6 minutes on each side.
3. Garnish on serving plate, as desired.

Hearth Method:

1. Preheat gridiron over hot coals and grease with suet.
2. Broil 4 minutes over hot coals.
3. Lift fish, grease gridiron, and turn fish to cook other side over fresh coals for 4 minutes.
4. Garnish on serving plate, as desired.

Servings: 1 per pound of whole fish
1 per ¾ pound trimmed fish
1 per ¼ pound fish steak

Salt Fish with Gravy

"Salt fish should be put in a deep plate, with just water enough to cover it, the night before you intend to cook it. It should not be boiled an instant; boiling renders it hard. It should lie in scalding hot water two or three hours. The less water is used, and the more fish is cooked at once, the better. Water thickened with flour and water while boiling, with sweet butter put in to melt, is the common sauce, It is more economical to cut salt pork into small bits, and fry it till the pork is brown and crispy. It should not be done too fast, lest the sweetness be scorched out."

1 lb. salt cod
Hot water to cover fish

GRAVY:
2 tbl. flour
2 oz. salt pork

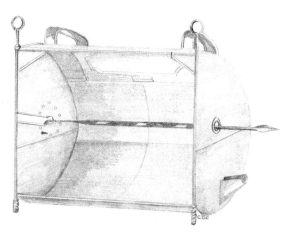

Tin Kitchen

Modern Method:

1. Soak cod in cold water overnight.
2. Place fish in a skillet and just cover with boiling water. Cook over low heat, but do not bring to a boil. Cook for 10-15 minutes, or until fish flakes easily with a fork.
3. To prepare gravy, cut salt pork into thin slices and fry until crisp. Add flour and blend well. Add 1 cup of the water in which fish cooked and cook until thickened. Add fish and heat before serving.

Hearth Method:

1. Follow Step 1 of the recipe above.
2. Use a pan or bowl placed on a trivet over coals in front of the fire. Put in fish, cover with boiling water and cover cooking container. Change coals from time to time. A small amount of fish will flake in about 15 minutes; more fish will take longer.
3. Follow Step 3 in the recipe above, using a skillet over hot coals.

Serving suggestion from Mrs. Child: "Salt fish needs plenty of vegetables such as onions, beets, carrots &c."

Servings: 4

Fish Chowder

"Four pounds of fish are enough to make a chowder for four or five people; half a dozen slices of salt pork in the bottom of the pot; hang it high, so that the pork may not burn; take it out when done very brown; put in a layer of fish, cut in lengthwise slices, then a layer formed of crackers, small or sliced onions, and potatoes sliced as thin as a four-pence, mixed with pieces of pork you have fried; then a layer of fish again, and so on. Six crackers are enough. Strew a little salt and pepper over each layer; over the whole pour a bowl-full of flour and water, enough to come up even with the surface of what you have in the pot. A sliced lemon adds to the flavor. A cup of tomato catsup is very excellent. Some people put in a cup of beer. A few clams are a pleasant addition. It should be covered so as not to let a particle of steam escape, if possible. Do not open it, except when nearly done, to taste if it be well seasoned."

4 lb. fish
4 large potatoes
4 large onions
12 common crackers
6 slices salt pork
4 tsp. salt
4 tsp. pepper
⅓ cup flour
4-5 cups water
For a different flavor, add one quarter of the following
    with each layer:
Sliced lemon
1 cup catsup (recipe on page 218)
1 doz. cooked clams
1 cup dark beer

Modern Method:

1. Cut potatoes and onions into thin slices, slice fish, and split crackers.
2. Using a large heavy kettle, fry slices of salt pork until browned and remove crisped pork.
3. Leave fat in kettle. Build the first layer with 1 pound of fish, one quarter of the sliced potatoes, onions, and pork scraps, three split crackers, 1 teaspoon of salt, 1 teaspoon of pepper. Repeat until all ingredients are layered in soup kettle.
4. Blend flour and 1 cup of water to make a smooth paste. Stir in remaining water and pour this mixture over fish layers until covered.
5. Cover the pot and heat slowly until contents simmer. In 30-45 minutes, remove the lid to test that the potatoes are done, and correct the seasonings, if necessary.

Hearth Method:

1. Follow Step 1 of the recipe above.
2. Follow Step 2 of the recipe above; using a large hanging pot over moderate heat.
3. Follow Steps 3 and 4 of the recipe above.
4. Cover the pot with a pie plate or foil, if it does not have a lid. Heat over moderate fire for 30-45 minutes, remove the lid to test that the potatoes are done, and correct the seasonings, if necessary.

Servings: 4-5

Fish Balls

"Salt fish mashed with potatoes, with good butter or pork scraps to moisten it, is nicer the second day than it was the first. The fish should be minced very fine while it is warm. After it has gotten cold and dry it is difficult to do it nicely. There is no way of preparing salt fish for breakfast, so nice as to roll it up in little balls, after it is mixed with mashed potatoes dip it into an egg, and fry it brown."

1 cup leftover fish, mashed while still warm
½-1 cup mashed potatoes
1 egg
¼ cup bacon fat or other fat for frying

Modern Method:

1. Mash potatoes and fish together. Form into balls using about 1 teaspoon of mixture for each ball.
2. When ready to cook, roll balls in beaten egg to coat them.
3. Heat fat in a skillet. Add fish balls and fry for 10-15 minutes, to heat through, stirring frequently.

Hearth Method:

1. Follow Steps 1 and 2 in the recipe above.
2. Follow Step 3 in the recipe above, using a hanging skillet over hot coals.

Yield: 35-40

Fish — codfish balls is a good dish for breakfast in the winter season.

— Sarah J. Hale, *The Way to Live Well and Be Well While We Live*, (Philadelphia, 1839)

Poached Fish

"A common sized cod-fish should be put in when the water is boiling hot, and boil about twenty minutes. Haddock is not as good for boiling as cod; it takes about the same time to boil.

"A piece of halibut which weighs four pounds is a large dinner for a family of six or seven. It should boil forty minutes. No fish put in till the water boils. Melted butter for sauce."

A large fillet of fish
Boiling water
2 tbl. melted butter for each serving of fish, optional
A Most Delicious Salad Sauce, optional (recipe on
page 103)

Modern Method:

1. Bring water to the boil in a large fish boiler or roasting pan.
2. Slip fish gently into the water and simmer from 5-8 minutes to the pound, depending on the thickness of the fish.
3. Serve with butter or "A Most Delicious Salad Sauce."

Hearth Method:

1. Follow Steps 1-3 in the recipe above, using a large kettle or very deep skillet over moderate heat.

Servings: 2 per pound

Clams with Broth

"Clams should boil about fifteen minutes in their own water; no other need be added except a spoonful to keep the bottom shells from burning. It is easy to tell when they are done, by the shells starting wide open. After they are done, they should be taken from the shells, washed thoroughly in their own water, and put in a stewing pan. The water should then be strained through a cloth, so as to get out all the grit; the clams should be simmered in it ten or fifteen minutes; a little thickening of flour and water added; half a dozen slices of toasted bread or cracker; and pepper, vinegar and butter to your taste. Salt is not needed."

3-4 doz. clams, in shells, 6-8 per person
Water to cover bottom of cooking pot
¼ cup of flour
¼ cup of butter or cream
6 slices of toast or 6 common crackers split in half
Pepper and vinegar to taste

Modern Method:

1. Cover bottom of pot with ½ inch of water to prevent clams on the bottom from burning.
2. Add clams and boil 15 minutes or until all shells open.
3. Remove clams from pot and shell. Rinse clams thoroughly in water in which they were cooked. Strain this water through cheesecloth to remove grit. Clean cooking pot.
4. Return clams and strained water to pot. Stir in paste of flour and butter or cream and bring almost to a boil.
5. Add pepper and vinegar to taste. Serve with toast or crackers.

Hearth Method:

1. Cover bottom of hanging kettle with ½ inch of water.
2. Add clams and hang over moderate to high heat. Boil 15 minutes or until all shells are open. Remove pot from fire.
3. Follow Step 3 in the recipe above.
4. Return clams and strained water to pot. Stir in paste made of flour and butter or cream. Hang over moderate fire 15 minutes or until it almost comes to the boil.
5. Follow Step 5 in the recipe above.

Servings: 6

Tea Kettle

Escalloped Oysters

"Put crumbled bread around the sides and bottom of a buttered dish. Put oysters in a skillet, and let the heat just strike them through; then take them out of the shells, and rinse them thoroughly in the water they have stewed in. Put half of them on the layer of crumbled bread, and season with mace and pepper; cover them with crumbs of bread and bits of butter; put in the rest of the oysters, season and cover them in the same way. Strain their liquor, and pour over. If you fear they will be too salty, put fresh water instead. Bake fifteen or twenty minutes."

2 doz. oysters or two 8-oz. cans
1 cup soft bread crumbs: rye, three-grain, etc.
¼ tsp. mace
½ tsp. pepper
2 tbl. butter

Modern Method:

1. Butter a 9-inch pie plate or other shallow baking dish. Press half the bread crumbs onto the buttered surface.
2. If fresh oysters are used, place them in a skillet with 1 cup of water and cook over low heat until shells open. Reserve cooking liquid. Remove oysters from the shell and arrange half on the crumbs in the dish. Season with half the mace and pepper; dot with 1 tablespoon of butter.
3. Cover with crumbs, then add the remaining oysters, mace, pepper, and butter. Strain the cooking liquid and pour over the contents of the baking dish.
4. Bake in a 350° oven for 15-20 minutes.

Hearth Method:

1. Follow Step 1 in the recipe above.

2. Follow Steps 2 and 3 in the recipe above, using a hanging skillet.
3. Bake in a brick oven or a bake-kettle with coals underneath for 20-25 minutes.

Servings: 6-8

Peas

"Dried peas need not be soaked overnight. They should be stewed slowly four or five hours in considerable water with a piece of pork. The older beans and peas are, the longer they should cook."

1 lb. dried peas
Water to cover peas
Meaty ham bone or ½ lb. pork

Modern Method:

1. Combine peas, water, and bone or meat in a heavy pot with a lid.
2. Bring to a boil, reduce heat and simmer 3-4 hours or until tender.

Hearth Method:

1. Follow Step 1 in the recipe above, using a hanging cooking pot with a cover.
2. Bring to a boil, reduce heat and simmer 3-4 hours. Add more boiling water if necessary before peas are tender.

Yield: 8 cups

Poached Eggs

"The beauty of a poached egg is for the yolk to be seen blushing through the white, which should only be just sufficiently hardened to form a transparent veil for the egg. Have some boiling water in a tea kettle; pass as much of it through a clean cloth as will half fill a stewpan; break the egg into a cup and when the water boils, remove the stewpan from the heat and gently slip the egg into it; it must stand until the white is set; then put it over a very moderate fire, and as soon as the water boils, the egg is ready; take it up with a slice, and neatly round off the ragged edges of the white; send them up on bread toasted on one side only, with or without butter."

4 fresh eggs
4 slices buttered toast

Modern Method:

1. Use a skillet or saucepan large enough to hold the four eggs. Add 2 inches of water and bring to a boil.
2. Break eggs individually into cups. When water simmers, remove from heat and slip eggs into the water.
3. When the transparent white of the egg turns white in color, return to heat until the water simmers again. When the white is firm and yolk is done to taste, remove egg with a slotted spoon.
4. Trim ragged edges if necessary. Serve on buttered toast.

Hearth Method:

1. Set up a spider or skillet over the fire. Fill to halfway mark with water and bring to a simmer.
2. Break eggs individually into cups. When water simmers, remove from direct heat and slip each egg gently into the water, taking care not to crowd the eggs.

3. When the transparent white of the egg turns white in color, add wood to the fire and return to heat until water simmers again. When the white is firm and yolk is done to taste, remove with a slotted spoon.
4. Follow Step 4 in the recipe above.

Servings: 4

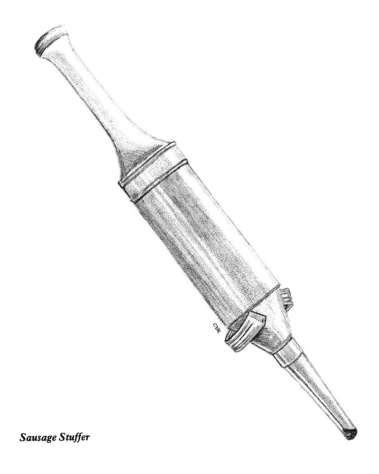

Sausage Stuffer

Omelet

"The following receipt is the basis of all omelets, of which you may make an endless variety. Break eight or ten eggs into a pan, add pepper, salt and a spoonful of cold water, beat them up with a whisk; in the meantime put some fresh butter into a frying pan, when it is quite melted and nearly boiling, put in the eggs, &c with a skimmer; as it is frying, take up the edges, that they may be properly done; when cooked, double it; serve very hot."

8-10 eggs
1 tsp. salt
½ tsp. pepper
3 tbl. butter
1 tbl. cold water
Optional:
    ½ cup chopped fresh parsley
    1 small chopped onion, fried until transculent
    ½ cup ham, chopped
    ½ cup tongue, chopped
    ¼ cup anchovy, chopped
    ½ doz. oysters, chopped
    1 tbl. chopped chives

Modern Method:

1. Beat eggs, water, salt and pepper until well blended.
2. Add one or more desired optional ingredients.
3. Melt butter in a skillet.
4. Pour egg mixture into melted butter. As edges cook, lift them and tilt skillet to allow uncooked egg to run underneath, until the egg is firm.
5. When cooked, fold in half and flip on to a warm plate. Serve hot.

Hearth Method:

1. Follow Steps 1 and 2 in the recipe above.
2. Melt butter in a hanging skillet over a moderate to low fire.
3. Follow Steps 4 and 5 in the recipe above.

Servings: 6-8

Beyond the woods and the open fronting space, in boggy regions when entering horses must wear the clumsy, square, wooden mud-shoes, was the meadow, the place of turtles, water snakes, muskrats and of historic beavers.

There we could not venture, but were glad that grandfather dared go after yellow-blossomed cowslip sprays, a dainty unsurpassed by young beet tops, "milk weed sprouts" or dandelion greens.

Alice J. Jones, *In Dover on the Charles* (Newport, Rhode Island, 1906)

Roasted Cheese

"Grate three ounces of fat cheese, mix it with the yolks of two eggs, four ounces of grated bread and three ounces of butter; beat the whole well in a mortar with a dessert spoonful of mustard and a little salt and pepper. Toast some bread, cut it into proper pieces; lay the paste, as above, thick upon them, put them into a Dutch oven covered with a dish till hot through, remove the dish and let the cheese brown a little. Serve as hot as possible."

1¼ cups grated cheddar or other hard cheese
2 hard-boiled egg yolks
2-3 cups soft bread crumbs
4 tbl. butter
1 tbl. mustard
Dash of salt & pepper
8 slices lightly toasted bread, or rusks (recipe on page 210)

Modern Method:

1. Blend cheese, mashed egg yolks, bread crumbs, butter, mustard, salt, and pepper.
2. Spread paste on toast. Bake in 350° oven covered for 15 minutes. Remove cover for last 5 minutes to brown the cheese.

Hearth Method:

1. Follow Step 1 in the recipe above.
2. Spread paste on toast. Place on pie plate covered with a plate in a Dutch oven. Place coals below Dutch oven and on the lid.
3. Bake 15 minutes. Remove cover from pie plate. Re-cover Dutch oven, heap fresh coals on cover for 5 minutes while cheese browns.

Servings: 4

A Most Delicious Salad Sauce

"Take the yolks of four hard-boiled eggs, rub them through a sieve, and add to them one teaspoonful of salt, stir well up, then add two tablespoonsful of made mustard, stir well up, then add by one spoonful at each time, six spoonsful of salad oil; mix this well together until it becomes as smooth as mustard, then put in one teaspoonful of anchovy sauce, and one gill of cream or new milk, and stir well together; and last of all put in by degrees some good vinegar to your own taste. Should you make it too sharp with vinegar, add one teaspoonful of fine white sugar in powder, this will soften it, and give it an excellent flavour. Bottle it for use. This will keep for any length of time in the hottest weather and is excellent with any kind of salad or boiled slaw, and is a fine relish with fish. Shake it well up before you put it on your salad."

4 hard-boiled egg yolks
1 tsp. salt
6 tbl. vegetable oil
2 tbl. prepared mustard
1 tsp. anchovy sauce, optional
¼ cup cream or whole milk
6 tsp. vinegar

Modern and Hearth Method:

1. Force the egg yolks through a strainer or grater.
2. Add salt and mustard, mix well.
3. Add oil, 1 tablespoonful at a time, blending between each addition.
4. Add anchovy sauce, if desired.
5. Add cream or milk and blend well.
6. Add vinegar 2 teaspoonfuls at a time.

Yield: 1 cup

Vegetables

Cooking Vegetables

"Put in no green vegetables till the water boils if you would keep all their sweetness. Asparagus should be boiled fifteen or twenty minutes; half an hour if old. Beets need to be boiled an hour and a half. Beet tops should be boiled twenty minutes. String beans should be boiled from twenty minutes to sixty, according to their age. Cabbages need to be boiled an hour. Corn should be boiled from twenty minutes to forty, according to age. Dandelions should be boiled half an hour or three quarters, according to age. Green peas should be boiled from twenty minutes to sixty, according to their age. Spinach should be boiled three or four minutes."

Modern Method:

1. Prepare vegetables for cooking.
2. Boil water in a large saucepan. Add vegetables. Simmer, covered, until tender.
3. Vegetables today are preferred crisp-tender rather than 'boiled to rags' as they would be if Mrs. Child's instructions were followed to the minute on a stove.

Asparagus: no more than 15 minutes.

Beans: about 20 minutes.

Beets: ½ hr. to 1 hour for young beets; they should be tender when pierced with a fork. 1-2 hours for old, large beets.

Greens: 20 minutes.

Cabbage: The old way was to cut into sections and boil for a long period. Instead, shred cabbage and boil 5 minutes.

Corn: Mrs. Child gives the timing for old-fashioned varieties of flint corn, grown for corn meal, rather than varieties of sweet corn. Sweet corn should be boiled or steamed 4-10 minutes.

Dandelions and other wild and edible greens: 35-40 minutes.

Peas: 10-15 minutes.

Hearth Method:

1. Follow Step 1 in the recipe above.
2. Boil water in a hanging iron pot. Add vegetables and return pot to moderate fire. Simmer covered until tender.
3. Follow Step 3 in the recipe above.

Iron Pot

Squash

"The lower part of a squash should be boiled half an hour and the neck pieces fifteen or twenty minutes longer."

Butternut or winter crookneck squash
1 tsp. salt
2 or more tbl. butter

Modern Method:

1. Cut the squash just below the neck. Scoop out seeds and peel. Chop squash into pieces of approximately the same size and thickness.
2. Put the neck pieces in a large pot of boiling water. Turn down heat and simmer for 15 minutes. Add remaining squash and cook 30 minutes, or until tender. Small pieces will cook more rapidly.
3. Remove from heat. Mash squash; add butter and salt. Stir squash to melt and blend butter.

Hearth Method:

1. Follow Step 1 in the recipe above.
2. Boil water in a large hanging pot. Add neck pieces and simmer over a moderate fire for 15 minutes. Add remaining squash and cook 30 minutes, or until tender. Small pieces will cook more rapidly.
3. Follow Step 3 in the recipe above.

Onions

"It is a good plan to boil onions in milk and water, it diminishes the strong taste of that vegetable. It is an excellent way of serving up onions, to chop them after they are boiled, and put them in a stewpan, with a little milk, butter, salt and pepper and let them stew about fifteen minutes. This gives them a fine flavor and they can be served up very hot."

1 lb. onions, white or brown, skinned
1¼ cup milk
2 tbl. butter
1 tsp. salt
1 tsp. pepper

Modern Method:

1. Peel onions. Cook whole in 1 inch of boiling water and ¼ cup milk.
2. Pierce onions with fork. When almost tender, about 20 minutes, remove from heat and drain.
3. Chop onions and return to heat in a clean pan, with remaining milk, butter, salt, and pepper. Simmer 15 minutes.

Hearth Method:

1. Follow Step 1 in the recipe above, using a hanging pot.
2. Follow Step 2 in the recipe above, removing pot from fire to check the onions for tenderness.
3. Chop onions. Wipe out pot or rinse with hot water. Return to cooking pot with butter, milk, salt, and pepper. Simmer for 15 minutes.

Servings: 4

Potatoes

"New potatoes should boil fifteen or twenty minutes, three quarters of an hour or an hour is not too much for large old potatoes; common sized ones half an hour. If you wish to have potatoes mealy, do not let them stop boiling for an instant and when they are done, turn the water off and let them steam for ten or twelve minutes over the fire. See they don't stay long enough to burn to the kettle. In Canada they cut the skin all off and put them in pans to be cooked over a stove by steam. Those who have eaten them, say they are mealy and white, looking like large snow-balls when brought upon the table."

Potatoes
Water to cover potatoes

Modern Method:

1. Wash potatoes well; do not peel or cut up.
2. Put potatoes into a heavy saucepan with a lid, and cover them with cold water. Bring to a boil, reduce heat, and cook 20-30 minutes or until almost soft. Time will depend on size of potato.
3. Pour off all the water and re-cover saucepan. Let potatoes steam for 15 minutes, or until rest of meal is ready. Remove skins before serving, if desired.

Hearth Method:

1. Follow Step 1 in the recipe above.
2. Put potatoes into a large hanging pot with a lid, and cover them with cold water. Bring to a boil directly over fire, cooking for about 20-30 minutes or until almost soft. Time will depend on size of potato.
3. Pour off the water. Put a clean cloth over potatoes, cover the pan and set it beside fire to steam for 15 minutes or

until rest of meal is ready.
4. Remove skins before serving, if desired.

Servings: 1 per potato

Fried Potatoes

"To fry potatoes take the skin off raw potatoes, slice and fry them, either in butter or thin batter."

Potatoes
Butter or other fat for frying
Thin pancake batter (recipe on page 186)

Modern Method:

1. Peel raw potatoes. Cut into thin slices.
2. Melt butter and add potatoes plain or after dipping in a thin pancake batter.
3. Fry 15-20 minutes or until crisp and brown.

Hearth Method:

1. Follow Steps 1-3 in the recipe above, using a hanging skillet over a hot fire.

Broiled Potatoes

"To broil potatoes parboil, then slice and broil them. Or parboil, and then set them whole on the gridiron over a very small fire, and when thoroughly done, send them up with their skins on."

Potatoes, of roughly equal size for convenience in cooking

Modern Method:

1. Bring a large pot of water to the boil. Add unpeeled potatoes individually, to keep water boiling. Cook for 10 minutes.
2. Cut potatoes into thick slices or leave them whole, if small.
3. Arrange on broiler or grill and broil 10 minutes on each side.

Hearth Method:

1. Follow Steps 1 and 2 in the recipe above.
2. Arrange on a gridiron, place over a slow fire and grill until crispy, 15 minutes or more depending on heat of coals beneath the gridiron.

Servings: 1 per potato

"The mechanics and manufacturers of the United States — their success or failure will be the barometer of our Nation's strength; if they fall not alone."

— *Ladies' Mirror* (July, 1833)

Mashed Potatoes

"To mash potatoes, boil the potatoes, peel them and break them to paste; then to two pounds of them, add a quarter of a pint of milk, a little salt and two ounces of butter and stir it all well over the fire. Either serve them in this manner; or place them on a dish in a form and then brown the top with a salamader.*"

4-6 potatoes, boiled in their jackets
1 cup milk
½ cup butter
Salt to taste

Modern Method:

1. Peel potatoes and mash well.
2. Add milk, butter, and a little salt and mix well.
3. If a browned top is desired, place pan under broiler for 10-15 minutes or until browned.

Hearth Method:

1. Follow Steps 1 and 2 in the recipe above.
2. If a browned top is desired, place in a heat-proof dish and use a preheated salamander or put into a preheated bake-kettle, cover and add coals to brown in about 10 minutes.

---

*A salamander is a circular iron plate which is heated and placed on top of a dish of food to be browned. An 1845 cookbook notes that "a kitchen shovel is sometimes substituted for it." — *Ed.*

Servings: 4

Potato Balls

"Add to each pound of potatoes mashed, a quarter of a pound of grated ham, or some sweet herbs or chopped parsley, an onion, salt, pepper and a little grated nutmeg or other spice with the yolk of a couple of eggs. Roll into balls, flour them or egg and bread-crumb them; fry them in clear drippings or brown them in a Dutch oven. An agreeable vegetable relish and a good supper dish."

1 lb. potatoes, or about 3 medium
4 oz. ham or 2 tsp. dried thyme, summer savory, or parsley
    or ½ cup fresh chopped herbs
1 medium onion, chopped fine
1 tsp. salt (less if ham is used)
½ tsp. pepper
¼ tsp. nutmeg
2 egg yolks
½ cup flour or 1 egg and ½ cup bread crumbs
Fat for frying

Modern Method:

1. Cook and mash potatoes.
2. If ham is used, chop or grate; add ham or herbs, chopped onion, salt, pepper, and nutmeg and blend well.
3. Beat egg yolks together with a fork and add to potato mixture.
4. Roll into balls, bite size, if for hors d'oeuvres, larger, if to be served with a meal. Dip into flour or egg and bread crumbs.
5. Preheat frying pan with ½-inch of fat. Add potato balls and fry until browned and heated through.

Hearth Method:

1. Follow Steps 1-4 of the recipe above.

2. Fry in ½ inch of fat in a hanging skillet or spider over hot coals, until browned or heated through, or place in a Dutch oven for 45 minutes with coals above and below.

Servings: 4

Roast Potatoes under Meat

"Half boil large potatoes, drain the water from them and put them under meat that is roasting and baste them with some of the dripping. When they are browned on one side, turn them and brown the other; send them up round the meat or in a small dish."

Potatoes, of roughly equal size for convenience in cooking

Modern Method:

1. Bring a large pot of water to the boil and add unpeeled potatoes individually, to keep water boiling. Cook for 10 minutes.
2. Add to pan in which beef or pork is roasting for last ½ hour of roasting time, and baste with pan juices. Turn after 15 minutes.

Hearth Method:

1. Follow Step 1 in the recipe above, using a large hanging pot.
2. Place under roasting meat in reflector oven for last 30-40 minutes of cooking. Turn after 15-20 minutes.

Servings: 1 per potato

Beet Root, Pickled

"Boil the roots tender, peel and cut them in what shape you please. Put them into a jar and pour over them a hot pickle of vinegar, pepper, ginger, and sliced horseradish. You may add capsicums and cayenne."

2 lb. beets
Water to cover beets
1 cup vinegar
8 peppercorns
½ tsp. ginger
1 tbl. horseradish
½ tsp. allspice or cayenne pepper, optional

Modern Method:

1. Cut tops off beets, leaving one inch of stem. Wash carefully. Put in saucepan, and half-cover beets with water. Cover pan.
2. Cook until tender, ¾ hour for young beets, 1-2 hours for large, older beets.
3. Pierce beets with fork. When tender, remove from heat, peel and slice.
4. To prepare the pickle, combine 1 cup cooking liquid, vinegar, peppercorns, ginger, and horseradish in a small pan. Bring to a boil, and pour over sliced beets. Discard remainder of cooking liquid.
5. Refrigerate 24 hours before serving to allow flavors to blend.

Hearth Method:

1. Follow Step 1 in the recipe above, using an uncovered hanging kettle over moderate fire. Add more boiling water, if necessary to keep beets covered.

2. Follow Step 2 in the recipe above.
3. Follow Step 3 in the recipe above, removing kettle from fire to check the beets for tenderness.
4. Follow Step 4 in the recipe above, using a small tin pan on a trivet over coals.
5. Follow Step 5 in the recipe above.

Servings: 8

Spider

Turnip Soup

"To make Turnip Soup pear [pare] a bunch of turnips (save out three or four) put them into a gallon of water with half an ounce of black pepper, an onion stuck with cloves, three blades of mace, half a nutmeg bruised, a good bunch of sweet herbs, and a large crust of bread. Boil them an hour and a half, then pass them through a sieve; clean a bunch of celery, cut it small and put it into your turnips and liquor with two of the turnips you saved and two young carrots cut in dice; cover it close and let it stew; then cut two turnips and carrots in dice, flour them, and fry them brown in butter with two large onions cut thin and fried likewise, put them all into your soup with some vermacelli. Let it boil softly until your celery is tender and your soup is good. Season it with salt to your palate."

[The full recipe makes enough soup for a good-sized crowd, using a gallon of water for the initial cooking of the turnip. We do not know how many turnips were in the bunch that the author was accustomed to using. Certainly the turnips grown were a much smaller variety than the waxed vegetables offered in the fall and winter. — *Ed.*]

3 large turnips or 12 small ones
½ gal. water
1 tsp. black pepper
2 onions, one large and one small
6 whole cloves
⅛ tsp. mace
¼ tsp. nutmeg
Herbs of your choice
6 stalks celery
2 carrots
2 tbl. flour
Butter for frying
Salt
1 cup vermicelli, optional

Modern Method:

1. Peel turnips. Cut one large or 4 small turnips into pieces, put in kettle with water, pepper, small onion stuck with cloves, mace, nutmeg, and herbs. Simmer for 1½ hours.
2. Puree boiled turnip in a blender or food mill.
3. Put the turnip puree into pot along with diced celery, one diced large turnip, and one diced carrot. Simmer for 20 minutes.
4. Dice remaining turnip and carrot, coat with flour and fry in butter. Slice and fry large onion. Add sauteed vegetables and vermicelli, if desired, to simmering ingredients and cook until celery is tender, about 20 minutes. Salt to taste.

Hearth Method:

1. Follow Step 1 in the recipe above, using a large hanging pot over high heat. When water boils, allow fire to become moderate to simmer vegetables.
2. Mash turnip with a wooden masher or a fork.
3. Follow Step 3 in the recipe above, over a very moderate fire.
4. Follow Step 4 in the recipe above, using a hanging skillet or in a spider over coals drawn out on the hearth.

Servings: 10

Onion Soup

"Take half a pound of Butter, put it into a Stew pan and set it on the fire, and let all the Butter melt, and boil untill it is done making a Noise; then have ready ten or a Dozen middling sized Onions, peeled and cut small, which throw into the Butter, and let them fry for a Quarter of an hour; then shake in a little Flour, and stir them round; shake your Pan and let them do a few minutes longer; when you must pour in a Quart or three Pints of boiling water; stir them round, and throw in a good piece of the upper Crust of the stalest Bread you have. Season with Salt to your Palate. Let it then stew or boil gently for ten Minutes observing to stir it often; after which take it off the Fire, and have ready the yolks of two Eggs beaten fine in a Spoonful of Vinegar, and then stir it gently and by Degrees into your Soup, mixing it well. This is a delicious Dish."

¼ lb. butter
10 medium onions, peeled and sliced thin
4 tbl. whole wheat flour
2 qt. boiling water
2 tbl. salt
1 tsp. pepper
Slice of bread
2 egg yolks
2 tsp. vinegar

Modern Method:

1. Melt butter in a large soup pot, add sliced onions and fry gently for 15 minutes. Onions should be translucent, and should not brown.
2. Sprinkle flour over onions, blend, and cook for 2 minutes.
3. Add boiling water gradually, stirring until soup thickens slightly. Add salt and pepper.

4. Simmer 20-30 minutes, or until serving time. Add bread 10 minutes before serving.
5. Immediately before serving, beat egg yolks with vinegar and stir gradually into the soup, mixing well.

Hearth Method:

1. Use a large hanging iron pot. Melt butter over heat. Swing pot toward hearth to add onions, stir to coat with butter and return to fire.
2. When translucent, pull pot toward hearth, add flour, blend and allow to cook, using the heat of the iron pot.
3. Add boiling water gradually, stirring until soup thickens slightly. Add salt and pepper. Push crane back over fire.
4. Follow Steps 4 and 5 in the recipe above.

Servings: 10

Vegetable Soup

"To ¼ lb. of fresh butter, boiling hot, add onions chopped very fine. When they are quite soft, throw in spinach, celery, kidney beans &c also chopped fine, with green peas, and any other vegetables that you can collect. Stir them well in the onions and butter till they begin to dry. Have ready a tea-kettle of boiling water, and pour about a pint at a time over your vegetables, till you have as much as you want. Serve up with bread or toast in the bottom of the dish. Pepper and salt to your taste."

1 cup chopped onion
¼ lb. spinach
3 stalks celery
1-2 cups cooked kidney beans
½ cup fresh green peas
Other vegetables, as available
Herbs of your choice
¼ lb. butter
1-2 qt. boiling water
1 tsp. salt
½ tsp. pepper
Toast slices or croutons

Modern Method:

1. Chop onion, spinach, celery, kidney beans, and other vegetables. Shell peas.
2. Melt butter and heat until bubbly.
3. Add onion and cook until soft. Add remaining vegetables and herbs and stir over heat for 1 minute.
4. Pour 2 cups boiling water over vegetables. Stir, add remaining water, using more for thin soup, less for thick.
5. Simmer 20-30 minutes. Correct seasoning. Put toast slices in serving dish and pour soup over or pass toast or croutons after serving.

Hearth Method:

1. Follow Steps 1 and 2 in the recipe above, using a large hanging pot.
2. Pull pot from heat toward hearth to add onions. Stir while cooking, using retained heat. Add remaining vegetables, stir to coat with butter and return crane and pot to heat of fire.
3. To add water, pull crane and pot toward hearth, add 2 cups of water at a time, stirring contents of pot between additions.
4. Follow Step 5 in the recipe above.

Servings: 10

The cellar, extending under the whole house, was a vast receptacle, . . . In the autumn, it was supplied with 3 barrels of beef, as many of pork, twenty barrels of cider, with numerous bins of potatoes, turnips, beets, carrots, and cabbages.

— S. G. Goodrich, *Recollections of a Lifetime*, 1857.

Stewed Tomatoes

"Tomatoes should be skinned by pouring boiling water over them. After they are skinned, they should be stewed half an hour, in tin (not cast iron, to avoid harmful interaction of the acids with iron), with a little salt, a small bit of butter and a spoonful of water to keep them from burning. This is a delicious vegetable. It is easily cultivated and yields a most abundant crop."

6 large tomatoes
1 qt. boiling water
1 tbl. water
1 tbl. butter
1 tsp. salt

Modern Method:

1. Place tomatoes in a bowl. Cover with boiling water. In a minute or two, the skins will slip off. Chop tomato.
2. Place in a saucepan with 1 tablespoon of water, butter and salt. Heat slowly, stirring occasionally, until cooked through, about 20 minutes.

Hearth Method:

1. Follow Step 1 in the recipe above.
2. If you have a tin-lined hanging pot use it, or else use a metal pan on a trivet over coals to stew tomatoes with water, butter and salt. Tomatoes will cook in 20-30 minutes.

Yield: 2 cups

Herbs

Rosemary Plant

Herbs

*"Sweet Herbs. Those in cookery are parsley, rocambole [leek],
winter savory, thyme, bay-leaf, basil, mint, borage, rosemary,
marjoram &c. The relishing herbs are tarragon, garden-cress,
chervil, burnet, and green mustard.*

*"All herbs should be gathered while in blossom. If left till they have
gone to seed, the strength goes into the seed. Those who have a
little patch of ground will do well to raise the most important
herbs, and those who have not, will do well to get them in quantities from some friend in the country; for apothecaries make a very
great profit upon them.*

*"All herbs should be carefully kept from the air. Herb tea to do any
good, should be made* very strong."

Recipes Using Herbs

Roast Veal, page 42
Veal with Pork and Greens, page 43
Pot Roast or A La Mode Beef, page 44
Minced Meat to Serve on Toast or as a Pie, page 46
Roast Lamb or Mutton, page 63
Pork Roast, page 56
Pork Sausage, page 55
Turkey, page 66
Stewed Chicken, with Broth to Serve Separately, page 72
Chicken Fricassee, brown, page 74
Chicken Fricassee, white, page 76
Chicken Broth (A Hearty Meal), page 80
Broiled Fish, page 87
Omelet, page 100
Beet Root, Pickled, page 116
Potato Balls, page 114
Turnip Soup, page 118
Vegetable Soup, page 122
Pickling to Preserve Vegetables, page 220

To Dry Herbs

Modern Method:

1. Pick flowering herbs on a dry day, and pinch off flowers. There are several methods of drying herbs:

a. To air-dry in a warm place, gather several stalks, tie with string, leaving a loop to hang on a nail or on a long cord extended between two nails.

b. To take advantage of the heat of the pilot light in a gas oven, arrange the herbs loosely on a cookie sheet and place in oven. Turn from time to time until dry.

c. Use a commercially available drying box, following manufacturer's directions.

Crush herbs when dry and store them in an airtight bottle or tin, with a label identifying the contents and date of preparation.

Hearth Method:

Pick flowering herbs on a dry day, and pinch off flowers. Lay them in the Dutch oven, near the fire. Rearrange from time to time, until the herbs thoroughly dry and the leaves crumble between the fingers. Crush and store in an airtight bottle or tin, with a label identifying the contents and date of preparation.

Herbs for Cooking

"**Sage** *is very useful for all kinds of stuffing. When dried and rubbed into powder it should be kept tight from air.*

"**Summer-savory** *is excellent to season soup, broth and sausages.*

"**Sweet-marjoram** *is the best of all herbs for broth and stuffing. Few people know how to keep the flavor of it. It should be gathered while in bud or blossom and dried in a tin-kitchen at a moderate distance from the fire. When dry, it should be immediately rubbed, sifted, and corked up in a bottle carefully."*

"Powder of fine herbs for flavoring Soups and Sauces when fresh herbs cannot be obtained. — Take dried parsley two ounces; of lemon-thyme, summer-savory, sweet marjoram and basil, one ounce each; dried lemon-peel one ounce; these must be dried thoroughly, pounded fine, the powder mixed, sifted, and bottled. You can add celery seeds if you like."

½ cup dried parsley
2 tbl. lemon-thyme
2 tbl. summer-savory
2 tbl. basil
2 tbl. dried lemon peel
2 tbl. celery seeds, optional

Modern and Hearth Methods:

1. Measure ingredients into a bowl.
2. Rub through a sieve or between the hands until finely crushed and well blended.
3. Store in a jar with a tight-fitting lid.

Yield: approximately 1 cup

Flavored Vinegars

"Basil Vinegar. Sweet basil is in full perfection about the middle of August. Fill a wide-mouthed bottle with the fresh green leaves of basil (these give much finer and more flavor than the fried,) and cover them with vinegar, or wine and let them steep for ten days; if you wish a very strong essence, strain the liquor, put it on some fresh leaves, and let them steep fourteen days or more. This is a very agreeable addition to sauces, soups and to the mixture usually made for salads.

"The flavor of the other sweet and savory herbs, celery and burnet &c may be procured, and preserved in the same manner by infusing them in wine or vinegar."

6 sprigs fresh basil, or 4-6 celery stalks with leaves, or dill, burnet, borage, lovage, tarragon, or rosemary
Quart jar with a lid
1 qt. white vinegar

Modern and Hearth Methods:

1. Wash freshly picked basil or other herb of choice and dry off as much moisture as possible.
2. Place basil or herbs in jar, but do not crowd. Fill with vinegar.
3. Store in a cool, dark place for 10-14 days. Strain through a cheesecloth into a clean jar for storage, or repeat steps 1 and 2 using fresh herbs and the steeped vinegar. After 10 days more, strain and discard herbs before use.

Yield: 1 quart

Salad Vinegar

"Vinegar for salads. Take of tarragon, savory, chives, eschalots, three ounces each; a handful of the tops of mint and balm, all dry and pounded; put into a wide-mouthed bottle, with a gallon of best vinegar; cork it close, set it in the sun and in a fornight strain off and squeeze the herbs; let it stand a day to settle, and then strain it through a filtering bag."

3 sprigs fresh tarragon
3 sprigs fresh savory
3 tbl. chives
½ cup sliced shallots
2 sprigs fresh mint
2 sprigs fresh lemon balm
1 gal. vinegar
Gallon jug
Cheesecloth
4 quart jars or bottles

Modern and Hearth Methods:

1. Combine herbs.
2. Remove approximately one cup of vinegar from gallon jug and put in herbs. Add more vinegar to fill, if necessary. Replace cap.
3. Leave in a warm place for two weeks.
4. Remove herbs from vinegar by straining and pressing out as much vinegar as possible.
5. Let settle for 24 hours.
6. Strain into 1-qt. jars or bottles for storage.

Yield: 4 quarts

Mustard

"Mustard is best when freshly made. Mix by degrees, the best ground mustard and a little fine salt with warm water; rub these a long time till perfectly smooth. Mild mustard. — Mix as above, but use milk instead of water and sugar instead of salt."

¼ cup powdered mustard
¼ tsp. salt, or 1 tsp. sugar
2-3 tbl. hot water, or milk

Modern and Hearth Methods:

1. Combine ingredients in a deep glass or ceramic dish. Blend until smooth with a spoon.

Herb Crusher

Herb Teas for Indigestion

*"**Thoroughwort** (boneset) is excellent for dyspepsy and every disorder occasioned by indigestion. **Succory** is a very valuable herb. The tea, sweetened with molasses, is good for the piles. It is a gentle and healthy physic, a preventive of dyspepsy, humors, inflammation and all the evils resulting from a restricted state of the system. Elderblow (**elderberry**) tea has a similar effect. It is cool and soothing and peculiarly efficacious either for babes or grown people, when the digestive powers are out of order. **Summer-savory** relieves the cholic. **Penny-royal** (mint) and **tansy** are good for the same purpose."*

TO BREW HERB TEA:
1-2 tsp. crushed herbs
¾ cup boiling water
Sugar, molasses, or honey

Pour water over crushed herb. Steep for 5 minutes, and strain into a cup or mug. Sweeten to taste.

Servings: 1

"Our Country — Rich as she is in the blessings of Civil
and Religious Liberty, May she never find her truest
wealth in the Virtues and Love of her children."

Puddings

A Note on Sugar

The recipes in *The American Frugal Housewife* were written for a time in which granulated sugar was not in everyday use. Therfore, except in the few recipes that specifically call for white (loaf) sugar, try using brown sugar or molasses. While we do not know exactly what brown sugar looked like in the early nineteenth century, the refining process removed the liquid from the molasses, resulting in a more crystallized product. By combining ½ cup of sugar with 2 tablespoons of molasses for each cup of sugar called for in the recipe, we feel we come close to reproducing the flavor.

The use of maple sugar in the past, especially in cooking, is a subject for speculation, for recipes calling for maple-products are practically nonexistent. We know that farmers who tapped their trees reduced the sap to sugar, rather than storing it as syrup, which spoils without refrigeration. This sugar was probably used in place of store-bought brown sugar in baking cakes and pies. Baking the sponge cake or cupcake recipes with maple sugar crystals would yield a delicious maple cake.

Sugar Cone and Nippers

Indian Pudding

"Indian pudding is good baked. Scald a quart of milk (skimmed milk will do) and stir in seven table spoonfuls of sifted Indian meal, a tea-spoonful of salt, a teacupful of molasses, and a great spoonful of ginger, or sifted cinnamon. Baked three or four hours. If you want whey, you must be sure and pour in a little cold milk, after it is all mixed."

1 qt. milk
7 tbl. cornmeal
1 tsp. salt
¾ cup molasses
1 tbl. ginger or 1 tbl. cinnamon
½ cup cold milk, optional

Modern Method:

1. Heat milk to boiling point. Add cornmeal and salt and stir well.
2. Add molasses and spices, stirring to blend.
3. Pour into buttered, 2-quart baking dish, and add cold milk, if desired.
4. Bake in 325° oven for 2 hours. Serve warm.

Hearth Method:

1. Heat milk in a shallow pottery baking dish on a trivet over coals. Add cornmeal and salt and stir well.
2. Remove from heat. Add molasses and spices, stirring to blend.
3. Add ½ cup cold milk, if desired.
4. Bake 4-5 hours in the brick oven. (The long cooking period is necessary because the oven cools as time passes.) If a Dutch oven is used, bake 2-2½ hours. Add fresh coals two or three times. Serve warm.

Servings: 8

Custard Pudding *(A Sauce)*

"Custard puddings sufficiently good for common use can be made with five eggs to a quart of milk, sweetened with brown sugar, and spiced with cinnamon, or nutmeg, and very little salt. It is well to boil your milk, and set it away till it gets cold. Boiling milk enriches it so much that boiled skim-milk is about as good as new milk. A little cinnamon, or lemon peel, or peach leaves, if you do not dislike the taste, boiled in the milk, and afterwards strained from it, give a pleasant flavor. Bake fifteen or twenty minutes."

4 cups milk
1 stick cinnamon, optional
5 eggs
½ cup brown sugar
¼ tsp. nutmeg or cinnamon
¼ tsp. salt

Modern Method:

1. Scald milk with cinnamon stick and set aside until cool. When ready to proceed, remove cinnamon stick.
2. Beat eggs, add brown sugar, spices, salt, and cooled milk.
3. Pour into 2-quart baking dish. For best results, place baking dish in a pan of hot water in the oven. Bake in 325° oven for 1 hour, or until knife inserted near the middle comes out clean. It will continue cooking and become more firm as it cools. Serve cold.

Hearth Method:

1. In a shallow pan, scald milk and cinnamon stick on a trivet over coals. Set aside to cool. When ready to proceed, remove cinnamon stick.
3. Beat eggs with a fork or whisk. Add sugar, spices, salt, and cooled milk.

4. Pour into 2-quart baking dish. To bake, use a brick oven that has been preheated for one hour, or put custard in after other items, such as breads or cakes, have baked. Bake pudding 1 hour. If using a Dutch oven, do not preheat. Put coals on lid and underneath. Bake 45 minutes or until custard is set. It will continue cooking and become more firm as it cools. Serve cold.

Servings: 8

Earthenware Jars

Bird's Nest Pudding

"If you wish to make what is called 'Bird's nest puddings,' prepare your custard, — take eight or ten pleasant apples, pare them and dig out the core, but leave them whole, set them in a pudding dish, pour your custard over them, and bake them about thirty minutes."

6 apples
½ recipe for Custard Pudding

Modern Method:

1. Follow Steps 1 and 2 in the recipe on page 136.
2. Core the apples. Do not peel them. Place close together in a 9-in. baking dish or 9-in. pottery pie plate. Pour custard over apples.
3. Bake in 325° oven for 45 minutes or until set.

Hearth Method:

1. Follow Steps 1 and 2 in the recipe on page 136.
2. Follow Step 2 in the recipe above.
3. Bake in oven that has preheated for one hour or from which breads and cakes have already been removed. Bake 2 hours. If using a Dutch oven, do not preheat. Place coals beneath and on the lid. Bake 30-45 minutes or until custard is set.

Servings: 6

Cheap Custard *(A Sauce)*

"One quart of milk, boiled; when boiling, add three table spoonfuls of ground rice or rice that is boiled, mixed smooth and fine in cold milk, and one egg beaten; give it one boil up and sweeten to your taste; peach leaves or any spice you please, boiled in the milk."

4 cups milk
1 bay leaf or ½ stick cinnamon, optional
1 egg
3 tbl. rice flour, cornstarch, or cooked rice
⅓ to ½ cup sugar

Modern Method:

1. Heat 3½ cups of milk to the boiling point, with bay leaf or cinnamon stick, if desired.
2. In a large bowl, blend remaining milk with rice or cornstarch and sugar, add beaten egg.
3. Remove bay leaf or cinnamon stick from milk and add 1 cup of hot milk to the mixture in the bowl. Blend and pour mixture into plan containing the remainder of the milk.
4. Heat slowly, stirring often, until slightly thickened. It will not be firm.
5. Serve warm or cold as a sauce over fruit, puddings, or in a trifle.

Hearth Method:

1. Follow Step 1 in the recipe above, using a hanging pot over a moderate to hot fire.
2. Follow Steps 2 and 3 in the recipe above.
3. Heat slowly over moderate to slow fire, stirring often, until slightly thickened.
4. Follow Step 5 in the recipe above.

Yield: 4 cups

Rice Pudding

"If you have some rice left cold, break it up in a little warm milk, pour custard over it, and bake it as long as you should custard. It makes very good puddings and pies."

½ cup warm milk
1 cup cooked rice
½ recipe for Custard Pudding

Modern Method:

1. Combine milk and rice over heat. Break up rice with a fork, and heat gently until milk is absorbed.
2. Follow Steps 1 and 2 of the recipe on page 136.
3. Place rice in baking dish and cover with custard. Bake in 325° oven for 30-40 minutes.

Hearth Method:

1. Combine milk and rice in baking dish set on a trivet over coals. Break up rice with a fork and heat gently until milk is absorbed.
2. Follow Steps 1 and 2 of the recipe on page 136.
3. Pour custard over rice. Set baking dish in a Dutch oven that has not been preheated. Place coals above and below and bake about 45 minutes.

Servings: 6

Rice Pudding with Fruit

"Swell the rice with a very little milk over the fire; then mix fruit of any kind with it — currants, gooseberries scalded, pared and quartered apples; put one egg in to bind the rice; boil it well, and serve it with sugar, beat together, with nutmeg, or mace."

¾ cup uncooked rice (not quick cooking)
3 cups milk
1 egg
1 cup fresh or dried fruit: currants, gooseberries, apples
pared and quartered, or raisins
⅓ cup brown sugar, less if dried fruits are used
2 tbl. brown sugar
1 tsp. nutmeg

Modern Method:

1. Put rice and milk in a saucepan. Cover and simmer slowly until rice is soft and liquid is absorbed, about 15-20 minutes.
2. Stir in beaten egg, fruit, and brown sugar and cook for 5 minutes or until thickened.
3. Combine remaining sugar and nutmeg. Serve pudding warm with nutmeg sugar.

Hearth Method:

1. Cook rice in milk in a hanging pot over a slow fire until rice is soft and liquid is absorbed, about 45 minutes.
2. Add beaten egg, fruit, and brown sugar and cook 5-10 minutes or until thickened.
3. Combine remaining sugar and nutmeg. Serve pudding warm with nutmeg sugar.

Servings: 6

Quaking Plum Pudding

"Take slices of light bread and spread them thin with butter, and lay in the pudding dish layers of bread and raisins, within an inch of the top; then take five eggs and beat them well, and mix them with a quart of milk, and pour it over the pudding; add salt and spice to suit your taste; you may put in a cup of sugar, and eat it with butter, or you may omit the sugar, and serve it up with sweet sauce. Bake it twenty or twenty-five minutes. Before you use the raisins, boil them in a very little water, and put it all in."

1 cup raisins
½ cup water or brandy
½ loaf rye bread with a firm crust
¼-½ cup butter
5 eggs
4 cups milk
½ tsp. salt
1 tsp. cinnamon
¼ tsp. freshly grated nutmeg

Modern Method:

1. Cook raisins in water or brandy for 15 minutes.
2. Slice bread, butter slices, line a 2-quart baking dish with a layer of slices.
3. Sprinkle with raisins. Continue to build layers until all bread and raisins are used.
4. Beat eggs, add milk and remaining ingredients. Pour over bread.
5. Bake 1 hour in 350° oven.

Hearth Method:

1. Cook raisins and water or brandy in a small pan on a trivet

over coals near the fire for 15-20 minutes or until raisins are plump.
2. Follow Steps 2-4 in the recipe above.
3. Bake in a preheated Dutch oven up to an hour. Cooking time will vary depending on the shape and thickness of the baking dish. If it is cooking very slowly after 45 minutes, change the coals above and beneath the Dutch oven.

Servings: 8

Herb and Spice Box

Hasty Pudding

"Boil water, a quart, three pints, or two quarts, according to the size of your family; sift your meal, stir five or six spoonfuls of it thoroughly into a bowl of water; when the water in the kettle boils, pour into it the contents of the bowl; stir it well, and let it boil up thick; put in salt to suit your own taste, then stand over the kettle, and sprinkle in meal, handful after handful, stirring it very thoroughly all the time, and letting it boil between whiles. When it is so thick that you stir it with great difficulty, it is about right. It takes about half an hour's cooking. Eat it with milk or molasses. Either Indian meal or rye meal may be used. If the system is in a restricted state, nothing can be better than rye hasty pudding and West India molasses. This diet would save many a one the horrors of dyspepsia."

1 cup sifted cornmeal
4¼ cups water
½ tsp. salt
Molasses or maple syrup
Milk
Butter

Modern Method:

1. Stir 3 tbl. cornmeal into ¼ cup water.
2. Boil remaining water, stir in cornmeal and water mixture. Let mixture come to a boil. Add salt.
3. Stirring constantly, add remaining cornmeal ¼ cup at a time, letting pudding come to a boil between additions.
4. Serve pudding hot with molasses and milk; when cold, cut leftovers into slices and fry in butter or lard. Serve for breakfast with butter and maple syrup or molasses.

Hearth Method:

1. Follow Step 1 in the recipe above.

2. Boil remaining water in a small hanging pot. Pull crane and pot from high heat. Stir in cornmeal and water mixture. Return to fire and bring to a boil. Add salt.
3. Pull crane and pot toward hearth. Add remaining cornmeal ¼ cup at a time, stirring to blend and returning to fire until mixture boils after each addition. This will take about ½ hour.
4. Serve pudding hot with molasses and milk.
5. When cold, cut leftovers into slices to fry in butter or lard. Melt butter in a hanging griddle over moderate fire. Pull away from heat to put slices into pan and then return to heat, until browned and ready to be turned. Serve for breakfast with butter and maple syrup or molasses.

Servings: 10-12

There was always a Fast Day, which I am afraid most of us younger ones regarded merely as a day when we were to eat unlimited quantities of molasses – gingerbread instead of sitting down to our regular meals.

— Lucy Larcom, *A New England Girlhood*, (1889)

A George Pudding

"Boil very tender a handful of whole rice in a small quantity of milk with a large piece of lemonpeel. Let it drain; then mix with it a dozen of good sized apples, boiled to a pulp, and as dry as possible. Add a glass of white wine, the yolks of five eggs, and two ounces of orange and citron cut thin; make it pretty sweet. Line a mould or basin with a very good paste: beat the five whites of the eggs to a very strong froth and mix with the other ingredients: fill the mould, and bake it of a fine brown color. Serve it with the bottom upward, with the following sauce: two glasses of wine, a spoonful of sugar, the yolk of two eggs, and a bit of butter as large as a walnut: simmer without boiling, and pour to and from the saucepan, till of a proper thickness, and put in the dish."

FILLING:
1 lemon
⅓ cup uncooked rice (not quick cooking)
1 cup milk
6 baking apples or 2 cups applesauce (recipe on page 216)
¼ cup white wine
3 eggs
½ cup citron or preserved orange peel, optional
½ cup sugar

CRUST:
¼ cup butter
1 cup flour
1 egg
3 tbl. water

SAUCE:
½ cup sherry, madeira, or apple cider
1 tbl. brown sugar
2 egg yolks
1 tbl. butter

Modern Method:

1. Cut lemon into thin slices and remove seeds. Combine rice, lemon slices, and milk in a saucepan. Cook covered over low heat for 45 minutes, or until rice is soft and milk is absorbed.
2. Make crust tó line 9-inch pie plate or 1¾-quart oven-proof bowl. Cut butter into flour, and add egg beaten with water. Roll out pie crust and line the dish.
3. Peel, core, and chop apples, or use applesauce.
4. When rice is cooked, mix the apples and remaining ingredients with the rice, and spoon into prepared dish.
5. Bake 1 hour at 375°.
6. Just before serving, combine the wine or cider, brown sugar, beaten egg yolks, and butter in a small saucepan over low heat. Simmer until blended and thickened.
7. Invert cooled pudding onto serving plate and top with sauce.

Hearth Method:

1. Cut lemon into thin slices and remove seeds. Combine rice, lemon slices, and milk in a small hanging pot. Cook over a slow fire or close to the crane if fire is hot, so that milk does not curdle. Cook until rice is soft and milk is absorbed.
2. Follow Steps 2-4 in the recipe above.
3. Bake in preheated Dutch oven for 1 hour, 1½ hours in moderate bake-oven.
4. Follow Step 6 in the recipe above, using a small pan on a trivet over coals.
5. Follow step 7 in the recipe above.

Servings: 8

Lemon Pudding

"Grate the rind of two fresh lemons, being careful not to grate any off the white part. Squeeze the juice out of the lemons, and strain it, to separate it from the seeds. Mix it with six large spoonfuls of fine white sugar. Take a quart of milk, and mix it with the rind of the lemons, a couple of table-spoonsful of pounded crackers, and a table-spoonful of melted butter. Beat six eggs to a froth, and stir them into the milk. Stir in the lemon-juice and sugar last, and then turn the whole into a pudding dish that has a lining and rim of puff paste. Bake it from twenty-five to thirty minutes. It should not be eaten till it is cold."

Juice and grated rind of 2 lemons
¾ cup white sugar
4 cups milk
2 tbl. bread crumbs
1 tbl. melted butter
6 eggs
½ recipe for Puff Pastry for Filled Turnovers

Modern Method:

1. Prepare recipe for Puff Pastry, page 168.
2. Mix milk, bread crumbs, and melted butter. Beat eggs until foamy and add to mixture.
3. Mix together lemon juice, rind, and sugar, and add to mixture, stirring until blended.
4. Pour into a pie plate or a 2-quart baking dish that has been lined with the pastry.
5. Bake for 1 hour or until set in a 350° oven. Cool before serving.

Hearth Method:

1. Follow Steps 1-4 in the recipe above, melting butter in a dish on a trivet over coals.
2. Bake in a preheated brick oven for 50-60 minutes or a preheated Dutch oven with coals above and beneath for 45 minutes.

Servings: 8

Common Sauce

"One sauce answers for common use for all sorts of pudding. Flour-and-water stirred into boiling water, sweetened to your taste with either molasses or sugar, according to your ideas of economy; a great spoonful of rosewater if you have it; butter half as big as a hen's egg. If you want to make it very nice, put in a glass of wine, and grate nutmeg over the top."

2 cups boiling water
2 tbl. flour
2 tbl. molasses or 2 tbl. sugar
1 tbl. butter
1 tbl. rose water or 1 tsp. vanilla
¼ cup wine, optional
¼ tsp. nutmeg

Modern Method:

1. Boil water in saucepan. Remove 2 tablespoons of water and add to flour to make a thick paste.
2. Stir flour and water paste into water in saucepan. Continue stirring until it thickens, and cook over low heat for 10 minutes.
3. Remove from heat. Add molasses, butter, rose water or vanilla, and wine, if desired. Stir to blend. Sprinkle nutmeg over before serving. Serve hot.

Hearth Method:

1. Follow Step 1 in the recipe above, using a tin pan.
2. Stir remaining water into paste, heating pan on a trivet over coals. Continue stirring until mixture thickens, and cook for 15-20 minutes.
3. Follow Step 3 in the recipe above.

Yield: 2 cups

Better Sauce

"When you wish a better sauce than common, take a quarter of a pound of butter and the same of sugar, mould them well together with your hand, add a little wine, if you choose. Make it into a lump, set it away to cool, and grate nutmeg over it."

¼ lb. butter
½ cup sugar
1 tbl. wine or brandy
¼ tsp. nutmeg

1. Cream butter and sugar.
2. Stir in wine or brandy, and mold into a ball. Chill for two hours or more.
3. Sprinkle grated nutmeg over hard sauce before serving.

Yield: ¾ cup

"May a millenium of Virtue, Peace and happiness, soon bless the whole family of man."

— Abner Gay (1815)

Orange Fool

"Mix the juice of three Seville oranges, three eggs well beaten, a pint of cream, a little nutmeg and cinnamon, and sweeten to your taste. Stir it over a gentle fire, and when it begins to thicken, put about the size of a small walnut of butter; keep it over the fire a few minutes longer, then pour it into a flat dish, and serve it to eat cold.

Juice of 3 large oranges* and 2 tbl. rind
3 eggs, well beaten
2 cups cream
⅛ tsp. nutmeg
⅛ tsp. cinnamon
⅔ cup white sugar
1 tbl. butter

Modern Method:

1. Combine ingredients in a heavy saucepan or double boiler.
2. Cook very slowly until it thickens slightly. Do not boil or it will curdle. Heat for no more than 25 minutes.
3. Chill in individual glass bowls or wine glasses. Serve cold.

Hearth Method:

1. Warm cream in a tin-lined pan on a trivet over coals near the fire or in a bowl set over a pan of hot water on the trivet.
2. Mix remaining ingredients and stir slowly into cream, adding fresh coals as needed to keep heat as even as possible. Stir until it thickens, about 15-20 minutes.
3. Follow Step 3 in the recipe above.

Servings: 6

* This has a very delicate orange flavor if Seville oranges are not used. Try using ⅔ cup of orange concentrate if you prefer a richer orange taste. — *Ed.*

Common Pies

Mince Pies

"Boil a tender, nice piece of beef — any piece that is clear from sinews and gristle; boil it till it is perfectly tender. When it is cold, chop it very fine, and be very careful to get out every particle of bone and gristle. The suet is sweeter and better to boil half an hour or more in the liquor the beef has been boiled in; but few people do this. Pare, core, and chop the apples fine. If you use raisins, stone them. If you use currants, wash and dry them at the fire. Two pounds of beef, after it is chopped; three quarters of a pound of suet; one pound and a quarter of sugar; three pounds of apples; two pounds of currants, or raisins. Put in a gill of brandy; lemon-brandy is better, if you have any prepared. Make it quite moist with new cider. I should not think a quart would be too much; the more moist the better, if it does not spill out into the oven. A very little pepper. If you use corn meat, or tongue, for pies, it should be well soaked, and boiled very tender. If you use fresh beef, salt is necessary in the seasoning. One ounce of cinnamon, one ounce of cloves. Two nutmegs add to the pleasantness of the flavor; and a bit of sweet butter put upon the top of each pie, makes them rich; but these are not necessary. Baked three quarters of an hour. If your apples are rather sweet, grate in a whole lemon."

1¼ lb. beef round or leftover roast
¼ lb. suet
1½ lb. apples
1 cup raisins or currants
½ cup white sugar
½ cup brown sugar
⅛ tsp. pepper
½ tsp. salt
2 tsp. cinnamon
1 tsp. clove
2 tsp. nutmeg
1 tbl. butter

¼ cup brandy
2 cups cider or apple juice
Double recipe for Pie Crust

Modern Method:

1. If uncooked meat is used, simmer beef 2-3 hours or until very tender, adding suet for last ½ hour of cooking.
2. When cooked, chop beef and suet very fine, into about ¼-inch pieces.
3. Pare, core, and chop apples to make 3 cups.
4. Mix beef, suet, apples, raisins or currants, white and brown sugars, spices, brandy, and cider or apple juice.
5. Follow Steps 1-6 in the recipe for Pie Crust, page 170.
6. Line pie plates with pastry, fill with half of meat mixture. Cover with top crusts, seal edges, slit holes on top for steam to escape. If desired, spread a thick layer of butter on pastry for flaky upper crust.
7. Bake ¾ hour in 400°-425° oven.

Hearth Method:

1. In a hanging kettle, simmer beef for 2 hours, adding suet for last ½ hour of cooking.
2. Following Steps 2-6 in the recipe above.
3. Set pies in metal pie plates on trivets. If pottery pie plates are used, set pies directly on floor of very hot bake oven. Or use a preheated Dutch oven with coals on lid and beneath. Change coals after 25 minutes to maintain a high temperature. Bake 45 minutes.

Yield: Two 9-inch pies

Pumpkin or Squash Pie

"For common family pumpkin pies, three eggs do very well to a quart of milk. Stew your pumpkin, and strain it through a sieve, or colander. Take out the seeds and pare the pumpkin, or squash, before you stew it; but do not scrape the inside; the part nearest the seed is the sweetest part of the squash. Stir in the stewed pumpkin, till it is as thick as you can stir it round rapidly and easily. If you want to make your pie richer, make it thinner, and add another egg. One egg to a quart of milk makes very decent pies. Sweeten it to your taste, with molasses or sugar; some pumpkins require more sweetening than others. Two tea-spoonfuls of salt; two great spoonfuls of sifted cinnamon; one great spoonful of ginger. Ginger will answer very well alone for spice, if you use enough of it. The outside of a lemon grated in is nice. The more eggs, the better the pie; some put an egg to a gill of milk. This should bake from forty to fifty minutes, and even ten minutes longer, if very deep."

Small pumpkin or squash
2 eggs, or 1 or 2 more "to make your pie richer"
2 cups milk (if you add eggs, reduce milk by ¼-½ cup)
½ cup molasses
Dash of salt
2 tbl. cinnamon
1 tbl. ginger
Peel of ½ lemon, grated
½ recipe for Pie Crust

Modern Method:

1. Cut up the pumpkin or squash, remove seeds and pare the outside rind. Simmer in a covered saucepan in a small amount of water until tender. Drain water and discard.
2. While pumpkin or squash cooks, prepare Pie Crust, page 170.

3. Force pumpkin through a sieve or use a food mill. Measure 2 cups puree for each pie. Remainder may be frozen or dried for future use.
4. Beat eggs and add milk. When blended, add pumpkin, molasses, salt, cinnamon, ginger, and lemon, and stir well.
5. Pour into pie shell in 9-inch pie plate. Bake in 400° oven for 15 minutes, then turn down to 375° for 30 minutes or until set. Cool before serving.

Hearth Method:

1. Cut up pumpkin, remove seeds and pare the outside rind. Simmer, covered with water in a hanging kettle over a moderate fire until tender. Take out pumpkin and discard cooking water.
2. While pumpkin or squash cooks, prepare Pie Crust, page 170.
3. Follow Steps 3 and 4 in the recipe above.
4. Pour into pie shell in a 9-inch pottery pie plate. Bake 50-60 minutes in a hot brick oven. Place the pie plate on a trivet, or bake 50-60 minutes in a pre-heated Dutch oven with coals on lid and beneath. Coals will not have to be changed.

Yield: one 9-inch pie

Cranberry Pie

"Cranberry pies need very little spice. A little nutmeg, or cinnamon, improves them. They need a great deal of sweetening. It is well to stew the sweetening with them; at least a part of it. It is easy to add, if you find them too sour for your taste. When cranberries are strained, and added to about their own weight in sugar, they make very delicious tarts. No upper crust."

½ recipe for Pie Crust
1 lb. whole cranberries
2-3 cups brown sugar
2 cups water
¼ tsp. nutmeg or cinnamon

Modern Method:

1. Follow steps 1-6 in the recipe for Pie Crust, page 170.
2. Prepare pie crust in a 9-inch pie plate or as 12-16 individual tarts. Bake for 20 minutes.
3. While crust bakes, combine cranberries, 2 cups brown sugar, and 2 cups water in saucepan. Simmer until cranberries pop and syrup has thickened. Add spice. Taste, and add sugar if the mixture seems too tart.
4. Spoon into the pie crust or tarts. Bake in 350° oven for 30 minutes.

Hearth Method:

1. Follow steps 1-6 in the recipe for Pie Crust, page 170, using half the recipe.
2. Prepare pie crust and bake for 20 minutes in a preheated Dutch oven. (Tin tart pans will not work in brick oven; use cast iron or a 9-inch pottery pie plate.)
3. Follow Step 3 in the recipe above, using a hanging kettle

or skillet over a moderate fire.
4. Spoon into the pie crust or tarts.
5. Bake in a moderate brick oven or preheated Dutch oven for 30 minutes.

Yield: one 9-inch pie or 12-16 tarts

Had we children been asked what we expected on Thanksgiving Day we should have clapped our hands and said that we expected a good dinner. As we had a good dinner every day of our lives this answer shows simply that children respect symbols and types. And indeed there were certain peculiarities in the Thanksgiving dinner which there were not on common days. For instance, there was always a great deal of talk about the Marlborough pies or the Marlborough pudding. To this hour, in any old and well-regulated family in New England, you will find there is a traditional method of making the Marlborough pie, which is a sort of lemon pie, and each good housekeeper thinks that her grandmother left a better receipt for Marlborough pie than anybody else did. We had Marlborough pies at other times, but we were sure to have them on Thanksgiving Day; and it ought to be said that there was no other day on which we had four kinds of pies on the table and plum pudding beside, not to say chicken pie. In those early days ice creams or sherbets or any other kickshaws of that variety would have been spurned from a Thanksgiving dinner.

— Edward Everett Hale, *A New England Boyhood*, 1893

Cherry Pie

"Cherry pies should be baked in a deep plate. Take the cherries from the stalks, lay them in a plate, and sprinkle a little sugar, and cinnamon, according to the sweetness of the cherries. Baked with a top and bottom crust."

Pie Crust
4 cups fresh cherries
1 tsp. cinnamon
⅔ cup brown sugar

Modern Method:

1. Follow Steps 1-6 in the recipe for Pie Crust on page 170, and line pie plate.
2. Remove stems and pits from cherries and arrange in pie plate.
3. Tuck in extra pieces of pastry around cherries.
4. Mix cinnamon and brown sugar and sprinkle over fruit.
5. Cover, and prick to allow steam to escape.
6. Bake in 375° oven for 50-60 minutes.

Hearth Method:

1. Follow Steps 1-5 in the recipe above, using a pottery pie plate.
2. Bake on a trivet in a hot oven for 50-60 minutes, or use a preheated Dutch oven with coals on lid and below.

Yield: one 9-inch pie

Carrot Pie

"Carrot pies are made like squash pies. The carrots should be boiled very tender, skinned and sifted. Both carrot pies and squash pies should be baked without an upper crust, in deep plates. To be baked an hour, in quite a hot oven."

1½ lb. carrots
3 eggs
2 cups milk
½ tsp. salt
2 tsp. cinnamon
1 tsp. ginger
Grated rind of ½ lemon
½ cup molasses
½ recipe for Pie Crust

Modern Method:

1. Cook carrots, peel, and mash or puree.
2. While carrots cook, prepare Pie Crust, page 170.
3. Mix together 1½-2 cups pureed carrots, beaten eggs, milk, salt, cinnamon, ginger, and lemon rind.
4. Pour into pie crust.
5. Bake one hour in 350° oven.

Hearth Method:

1. Follow Step 1 in the recipe above, using a hanging pot over a moderate fire.
2. Follow Steps 2-4 in the recipe above.
3. Bake pie on a trivet in moderate brick oven for 50-60 minutes, or bake in preheated Dutch oven with coals on lid and beneath for 50-60 minutes.

Yield: one 9-inch pie

Apple Pie

"When you make apple pies, stew your apples very little indeed; just strike them through, to make them tender. Some people do not stew them at all, but cut them up in very thin slices, and lay them in the crust. Pies made in this way may retain more of the spirit of the apple; but I do not think the seasoning mixes in as well. Put in sugar to your taste; it is impossible to make a precise rule, because apples vary so much in acidity. A very little salt, and a small piece of butter in each pie, makes them richer. Cloves and cinnamon are both suitable spice. Lemon-brandy and rose-water are both excellent. A wine-glass full of each is sufficient for three or four pies. If your apples lack spirit, grate in a whole lemon."

Pie Crust
6 cups apples, fresh or dried, or 2 cups applesauce (recipe on page 216)
½ cup brown sugar
½ tsp. cloves or cinnamon
1 tbl. butter
½ tsp. salt, optional
1 tbl. lemon peel, if apples are sweet
1 tbl. lemon brandy or rosewater, optional

Modern Method:

1. To prepare apples, follow one of these three methods:
   a. Peel and slice apples, toss with sugar and spice until all are coated.
   b. Peel and core whole apples, slice into rings. Put into saucepan with 1 inch of water on the bottom, sugar and spices. Stew for 10 minutes.
   c. Put dried apples in a bowl and cover with water. They will swell up in a couple of hours in a warm place. Put apples, a small amount of the water in which they soaked, sugar and spice into a saucepan and cook for 10 minutes.

2. Follow Steps 1-6 of the recipe for Pie Crust on page 170.
3. Line a 9-inch plate with pastry.
4. Arrange prepared apples in pie plate. Add juice if stewed. Dot with butter. Add salt, lemon peel, and brandy or rosewater, if desired. Cover with top crust, make slits to let steam escape.
5. Bake in 350° oven for 1 hour if stewed apples are used or 1¼ hours for uncooked fruit.

Hearth Method:

1. To prepare apples, follow one of these three methods:
    a. Peel and slice apples, toss with sugar and spice until all are coated.
    b. To stew apples, peel and core whole apples, slice into rings. Put in a small hanging kettle with 1 inch of water on the bottom, sugar and spices. Simmer over hot fire for 10 minutes.
    c. Put dried apples in a bowl of water to cover. They will swell up in a couple of hours if left in a warm place, such as on a trivet near the fire. Put apples, a small amount of the water in which they soaked, sugar and spice into a hanging kettle over a hot fire, and cook for about 10 minutes.
2. Follow Steps 2 and 3 of the recipe above.
3. Bake in a hot preheated brick oven for 50 minutes. Preheat Dutch oven and heap coals on lid and beneath and bake for about 50 minutes for a little longer.

Yield: one 9-inch pie

Rhubarb Stalks, or Persian Apple Pie

"Rhubarb stalks, or the Persian apple, is the earliest ingredient for pies, which the spring offers. The skin should be carefully stripped, and the stalks cut into small bits, and stewed very tender. These are dear pies, for they take an enormous quantity of sugar. Seasoned like apple pies. Always remember it is more easy to add seasoning than to diminish it."

8 cups rhubarb, cut in 1-inch pieces, peeled if desired
1¾ cup brown sugar, or 1 cup white and ¾ cup brown
¼ tsp. cloves
1 tsp. cinnamon
½ recipe for Pie Crust

Modern Method:

1. Combine rhubarb, sugar, and spices, and simmer ½ hour until tender. Heat must be very low so that sugar does not burn.
2. Follow Steps 1-6 in the recipe for Pie Crust, page 170.
3. Line a 9-inch pie plate with pastry.
4. Pour cooked fruit into crust.
5. Bake in 400° oven 40 minutes.

Hearth Method:

1. Follow Step 1 in the recipe above, using a hanging kettle over a very slow fire, or hanging high over the fire.
2. Follow Steps 2-4 in the recipe above.
3. Bake in a hot brick oven or preheated Dutch oven for 40 minutes, with coals on lid and beneath.

Yield: one 9-inch pie

Marlborough Pudding

"Grate enough apples to make 8 oz., add to this 8 oz. fine white sugar, 4 oz. butter, 6 eggs well beaten, the juice of 2 lemons, with the grated peel of one. Line a pie dish with fine puff paste, put the pudding in it and bake in a quick oven."

Juice and peel of 1 lemon (omit if using applesauce)
2 large fresh apples or 1 cup applesauce
1 cup sugar (use only ⅓ cup if applesauce is used)
3 eggs
½ cup butter
½ recipe for Puff Pastry for Filled Turnovers

Modern Method:

If fresh apples are used, follow Step 1. If using applesauce begin with Step 2.

1. Squeeze lemon and grate peel into large bowl. Grate apples into lemon juice and toss to coat apples to prevent darkening.
2. Pour sugar over fruit and mix well.
3. Follow Steps 1-4 in the recipe for Puff Pastry for Filled Turnovers, page 168. Line pie plate with pastry.
4. Beat eggs until light.
5. Cream butter until soft and add eggs, blending well.
6. Stir butter and egg mixture into sweetened fruit and spoon into deep, 8-inch pie plate.
7. Bake 15 minutes at 400°. Reduce heat to 350° and bake 45 minutes more or until a knife inserted in the center comes out clean. Cool before serving.

Hearth Method:

1. Follow Steps 1-6 in the recipe above.
2. Bake 1 hour in hot bake oven, or preheated Dutch oven, with coals on lid and below.

Yield: one 8-inch deep-dish pie

Apple Charlotte

"Cut a sufficient number of thin slices of white bread to cover the bottom and line the sides of a baking-dish, first rubbing it thickly with butter. Put thin slices of apples into the dish in layers, till the dish is full, strewing sugar and bits of butter between. In the meantime; soak as many thin slices of bread as will cover the whole, in warm milk; over which place a plate, and a weight, to keep the bread close upon the apples. Let it bake slowly for three hours."

8 slices stale bread
¾ cup milk
3 cups apple slices
½ cup sugar
1 tsp. cinnamon or nutmeg, if desired
2 tbl. butter

Modern Method:

1. Butter a 9-inch pie plate or a 1½-quart baking dish with a heavy lid.
2. Dip 4 slices of bread into milk and line the bottom and sides of the baking dish with the bread.
3. Layer apples, sugar, spice and dots of butter until dish is filled.
4. Dip remaining bread into milk and arrange on top of apples. Filling will be quite high.
5. Cover with lid or oven-proof plate to press down the top layers of apples and bread.
6. Bake in a 350° oven for ½ hour or a little more until apples are soft when tested with a knife. Serve hot or cold.

Hearth Method:

1. Follow Steps 1-5 in the recipe above.

2. Bake on a trivet in a moderate bake-oven or in a Dutch oven for ½ hour or a little more.

Servings: 8

Puff Pastry for Filled Turnovers

"Take an equal quantity of flour and butter, rub rather more than half the flour into one third of the butter, then add cold water to make it into a stiff paste. Make it round and roll it out. Dot half of the remaining butter over pastry, sift flour over it, roll up pastry, flour board and rolling pin, and roll it out. Repeat once or twice until all the butter is used.

"Roll out puff paste nearly a quarter of an inch thick and with a small saucer or a tin cutter of that size, cut it into round pieces; place upon one side raspberry or strawberry jam, or any sort of preserved fruit or stewed apples; wet the edges, fold over the other side, and press it round with the finger and thumb. Or cut the paste in the form of a diamond, lay on the fruit, and fold over the paste, so as to give it a triangular shape."

PASTRY:
2 cups butter
3½ cups whole-wheat flour, measured after sifting (see "A Note on Flour," page 173.)
½ cup cold water

1. Blend ⅔ cup butter and 2 cups of flour.
2. Add ½ cup cold water, stirring gradually.
3. Roll out on a floured board. Dot with half the remaining butter, sprinkle with ¾ cup of remaining flour, dusting some on rolling pin, and roll up like a jelly roll.
4. Roll this out and repeat to use up the flour and butter.

FILLING:
Jam or preserves of your choice. Try with filling for mince or cranberry pie

Modern Method:

1. Roll out puff pastry to ¼-inch thickness, cut into circles or diamonds.
2. Place a spoonful of jam, preserves, or other jelly on one side of pastry. Wet the edges and fold over to form a crescent or triangle. Seal firmly.
3. Bake at 400° for 8-10 minutes or until lightly browned.

Hearth Method:

1. Preheat oven for 2 hours.
2. Follow Steps 1 and 2 of the recipe above.
3. Bake for 10 minutes, or until lightly browned.

Servings: 20-24

Pie Crust

"To make pie crust for common use, a quarter of a pound of butter is enough for a half a pound of flour. Take out about a quarter part of the flour you intend to use, and lay it aside. Into the remainder of the flour rub butter thoroughly with your hands, until it is so short that a handful of it, clasped tight, will remain in a ball, without any tendency to fall in pieces. Then wet it with cold water, roll it out on a board, rub over the surface with flour, stick little lumps of butter all over it, sprinkle some flour over the butter, and roll the dough all up; flour the paste, and flour the rolling-pin; roll it lightly and quickly; flour it again; stick in bits of butter; do it up; flour the rolling-pin, and roll it quickly and lightly; and so on, till you have used up your butter. Always roll from you. Pie crust should be made as cold as possible, and set in a cool place; but be careful it does not freeze. Do not use more flour than you can help in sprinkling and rolling. The paste should not be rolled out more than three times; or it will not be flaky."

2 cups sifted whole-wheat flour or 3 cups rye flour, measured after sifting (see "A Note on Flour," page 172.)
½ cup butter
6 tbl. cold water

Modern Method and Hearth Method:

1. Measure and set aside ½ cup flour and 2 tbl. butter.
2. Rub the remaining butter into the flour.
3. Stir in cold water with a fork.
4. Roll dough out on well-floured board with a floured rolling pin, dot with 1 tbl. reserved butter, and sprinkle 1 tbl. reserved flour. Roll up the dough like a jelly roll. Flour lightly and roll to a ¼-inch thickness.
5. Repeat Step 4 twice, to use all butter and flour.
6. Use in a recipe or store in a cool place until needed.

Yield: two 9-inch pie crusts

Common Cakes

Common Cakes

"In all cakes where butter and eggs are used, the butter should be very faithfully rubbed into the flour and the eggs beat to a foam, before the ingredients are mixed."

A Note on Flour

When Mrs. Child wrote *The American Frugal Housewife* white flour was not in everyday use. In testing the recipes, we have found that the results are fine when today's unbleached white flour is used. However, the textures and flavors are richer when whole-wheat and rye flour are used, at least in part. Because the original directions just called for flour, we found that by using part whole-wheat or rye along with white flour, the results are lighter and more palatable and still within the spirit of the 150-year-old recipes. In making bread, Mrs. Child recommended using one-third each of rye, wheat, and cornmeal for the "nicest of all bread." This rule also holds for making cakes and pastries. Vary the proportions of rye and whole-wheat to white flour according to your family's preferences and what you have on hand.

Cup Cake

"Cup cake is about as good as pound cake, and is cheaper. One cup of butter, two cups of sugar, three cups of flour, and four eggs, well beat together, and baked in pans or cups. Bake twenty minutes, and no more."

1 cup butter
2 cups sugar
4 eggs
3 cups flour, measured after sifting

Modern Method:

1. Cream butter and sugar thoroughly.
2. Beat eggs and blend into creamed butter and sugar.
3. Add flour and beat in for 2 minutes.
4. Use cupcake, muffin pans or oven-proof cups, like custard cups. Grease and flour and fill each cup ½ to ⅔ full.
5. Bake at 375° for 20 minutes.

Hearth Method:

1. Follow Steps 1-3 in the recipe above.
2. Use cast-iron cupcake, muffin pans or oven-proof cups like custard cups. (Cupcakes will burn if tin muffin pans are used in a brick oven.) Grease and flour and fill each cup ½ to ⅔ full.
3. Bake for 20 minutes in a preheated brick oven or Dutch oven with coals below and on the lid.

Yield: 20-24 cupcakes

Gingerbread Cookies

"Take a tea-cupful of molasses, a tea-spoonful of saleratus dissolved in half a cup of boiling water, a teaspoonful of ginger, and flour to make it hard enough to roll. Bake it five minutes."

⅓ cup boiling water
1 tsp. baking soda
¾ cup molasses
1 tsp. ginger
2¼ cups sifted whole-wheat flour

Modern Method:

1. Pour boiling water into a large mixing bowl and add baking soda, then molasses. When mixed, add ginger.
2. Add flour gradually and work into a soft dough. Chill 15 minutes or more.
3. Take about half the dough at a time and roll out on a floured board. Cut into small circles or desired shapes.
4. Bake on a greased cookie sheet in a 350° oven for 8 minutes. Thick or large cookies will take a little longer.

Hearth Method:

1. Follow Steps 1-4 in the recipe above.
2. Bake on greased pottery plates; 5 minutes in a brick oven, slightly longer in a Dutch oven, changing coals after every second batch.

Yield: 30 cookies

Soft Gingerbread

"Six tea cups of flour, three of molasses, one of cream, one of butter, one table-spoonful of ginger and one of saleratus."

4½ cups flour
1 tbl. ginger
1 tbl. baking soda
¾ cup cream
2¼ cups molasses
¾ cup butter

Modern Method:

1. Sift together flour, ginger, and baking soda.
2. Cut butter into dry ingredients and blend thoroughly.
3. Stir in cream and molasses.
4. Grease two 8-inch or 9-inch square pans. Bake 45 minutes at 300°.

Hearth Method:

1. Follow Steps 1-3 in the recipe above.
2. Use greased pottery pie plates or cast-iron pans. Baking time in preheated brick oven or Dutch oven will range from 30-45 minutes depending on size of pan and depth of batter.

Servings: 12-18

Election Cake

"Old-fashioned election cake is made of four pounds of flour; three quarters of a pound of butter; four eggs; one pound of sugar; one pound of currants, or raisins if you choose; half a pint of good yeast; wet it with milk as soft as it can be and be moulded on a board. Set to rise over night in winter; in warm weather, three hours is usually enough for it to rise. A loaf, the size of common flour bread, should bake three quarters of an hour."

1 cup yeast or 2 pkg. yeast with 1 cup warm water and 1 tbl. sugar (see yeast recipe, page 202)
¾ cup butter
1 cup sugar
2 eggs
7-8 cups sifted flour
½ lb. currants or raisins
1 cup milk, or more

Modern Method:

1. If packaged yeast is used, mix water and sugar with yeast.
2. Cream butter and sugar. Add eggs, beating after each addition. Add yeast and blend well.
3. Stir in 4 cups flour and beat 1 minute.
4. Combine currants with 3 cups remaining flour and add to rest of batter. Batter will be stiff and flour may need to be worked in by hand. Add milk as required to make a soft, yet kneadable dough.
5. Sprinkle remaining flour on a board. Knead for 10 minutes.
6. Divide dough in half. Use 5" x 9" loaf pans or two 8-inch pie plates. Let rise in greased pans in a warm place for 3-5 hours or overnight in the refrigerator.
7. Bake in preheated 350° oven for 50 minutes.

Hearth Method:

1. Follow Steps 1-5 in the recipe above.
2. Divide dough in half. To bake in brick oven or Dutch oven, use cast-iron or ceramic pans, 5″ x 9″ loaf pans or two 8-inch pie plates. Set in front of the fire or in any warm place to rise. The cake will rise in 2 hours in front of the fire while the oven preheats. Allow 3-5 hours to rise in a less warm place or overnight in a cool place or refrigerator.
3. Bake in a hot preheated brick oven for 45 minutes.

Yield: two loaves or rounds

Old election, 'Lection Day as we called it, a lost holiday now, was a general training day, and it came at our most delightful season, the last of May. Lilacs and tulips were in bloom. . . . My mother always made Lection cake for us on that day. It was nothing but a kind of sweetened bread with a slice of egg and molasses on top; but we thought it delicious.

— Lucy Larcom, *A New England Girlhood*, Boston, 1889

Wedding Cake

"*Good common wedding cake may be made thus: Four pounds of flour, three pounds of butter, three pounds of sugar, four pounds of currants, two pounds of raisins, twenty-four eggs, half a pint of brandy, or lemon-brandy, one ounce of mace, and three nutmegs. A little molasses makes it dark colored, which is desirable. Half a pound of citron improves it; but is not necessary. To be baked two hours and a half, or three hours. After the oven is cleared, it is well to shut the door for eight or ten minutes, to let the violence of the heat subside, before cake or bread is put in.*

"*To make icing for your wedding cake, beat the whites of eggs to an entire froth, and to each egg add five teaspoonfuls of sifted loaf sugar, gradually; beat it a great while. Put it on when your cake is hot, or cold, as is most convenient. It will dry in a warm room, a short distance from a gentle fire, or in a warm oven.*"

[The full recipe will make 14 pounds of cake which can be baked in different size pans to build up a tiered wedding cake. This requires a very large bake oven or a combination of ovens and kettles. A very fruity and spicy cake with the combination of nutmeg and mace. — *Ed.*]

FULL RECIPE:
2 lb. raisins
1 cup brandy
12 cups flour
4 tbl. mace
2 tbl. grated nutmeg
4 lb. currants
8 oz. citron, optional
3 lb. butter
6 cups sugar
2 doz. eggs
½ cup molasses

Yield: 14 pounds of cake

¼ RECIPE:
½ lb. raisins
¼ cup brandy
3 cups flour
1 tbl. mace
2 tbl. nutmeg
1 lb. currants
2 oz. citron, optional
¾ lb. butter
1½ cups sugar
6 eggs
2 tbl. molasses

Modern Method:

1. Soak raisins in brandy overnight.
2. Sift flour before measuring. Sift flour with spices, add currants and citron, if desired.
3. Cream butter and sugar. Add eggs one at a time, beating to blend after each addition. Stir in molasses and any brandy that was not absorbed by the raisins. Stir in sifted flour with spices and fruits.
4. Grease two 5″ x 9″ loaf pans, three 8-inch round pans or one 10-inch tube pan.
5. Pour batter into greased pans and bake about 2 hours or a little more in 350° oven.

Hearth Method:

1. Follow Steps 1-3 in the recipe above.
2. Pour batter into three greased pottery or ceramic baking pans and bake 2¼ hours in a preheated hot bake-oven.

ICING:
3 egg whites
1 cup powdered granulated sugar (not superfine)

Modern and Hearth Methods:

1. Beat egg whites. Add sugar, beating until smooth and white.
2. Spread icing over slightly warm cake. It will harden *very* slowly. Set cake back into oven to begin drying as the oven cools down.

Yield: one 10-inch tube cake, or two 5″ x 9″ loaves,
    or three 8-inch layers

Sponge Cake

"The nicest way to make sponge cake, or diet-bread, is the weight of six eggs in sugar, the weight of four eggs in flour, a little rosewater. The whites and yolks should be beaten thoroughly and separately. The eggs and sugar should be well beaten together; but after the flour is sprinkled, it should not be stirred a moment longer than is necessary to mix it well; it should be poured into the pan, and got into the oven with all possible expedition. Twenty minutes is about long enough to bake. Not to be put in till some other articles have taken off the first few minutes of furious heat."

Mortar and Pestle

6 eggs, separated
2¼ cups sugar
2¼ cups flour, sifted [Try with rye flour! —*Ed.*]

Modern Method:

1. Beat egg whites until stiff.
2. Beat egg yolks, add sugar gradually, beating until thick and lemon colored.
3. Gently fold yolks into whites.
4. Sift flour over the batter and fold in gently.
5. Grease and flour two 8-inch or 9-inch layer cake pans or a 9-inch tube pan. Spoon batter into pan.
6. Bake at 375° for 50-55 minutes.

Hearth Method:

1. Follow Steps 1-4 in the recipe above.
2. Grease and flour three 8-inch or 9-inch pottery pie plates or 2 large, straight-sided ceramic baking dishes, such as a souffle dish. Spoon batter into plate or dish.
3. Bake in a hot brick oven for 45-50 minutes.

Yield: 2 8-inch or 9-inch layers or 1 9-inch tube cake.

Doughnuts

"For dough-nuts, take one pint of flour, half a pint of sugar, three eggs, a piece of butter as big as an egg, and a tea-spoonful of dissolved pearlash. When you have no eggs, a gill of lively emptings will do; but in that case, they must be made over night. Cinnamon, rose-water, or lemon-brandy, if you have it. If you use part lard instead of butter, add a little salt. Not put in till the fat is very hot. The more fat they are fried in, the less they will soak fat."

4 tbl. butter
1 cup sugar
3 eggs
2 cups flour
1 tsp. baking powder
1 tsp. cinnamon
Fat for deep frying

Modern Method:

1. Cream butter and sugar.
2. Add eggs one at a time and beat well.
3. Sift and measure flour, stir in baking powder and cinnamon.
4. Knead gently until ingredients are blended.
5. Pull dough apart and roll into 1-inch balls, no larger or centers will not cook before crust is thoroughly brown.
6. Preheat fat to 375° in an electric fryer or melt and warm fat on top of stove. The fat is hot enough when a small pinch of dough dropped in rises to the surface of the fat immediately.
7. Slip doughnuts carefully into the hot fat. Do not crowd. Turn when underside has browned. Drain on paper towels.

Hearth Method:

1. Follow Steps 1-5 in the recipe above.
2. Follow Step 6 in the recipe above, using a hanging skillet.
3. Follow Step 7 in the recipe above, pulling the skillet forward away from fire when putting doughnuts into the fat.

Yield: 4 dozen

Raised Doughnuts

⅔ cup hot water
1 pkg. yeast
2 tbl. sugar
4 tbl. butter
2 cups flour
1 cup sugar
1 tsp. cinnamon

Modern Methods:

1. Combine water, yeast, and 2 tablespoons of sugar.
2. Melt butter in yeast mixture. Add flour, sugar, and cinnamon.
3. Turn out onto floured board and knead for ½ minute.
4. Replace in bowl, cover and refrigerate overnight.
5. Follow Steps 6 and 7 in the recipe on page 182.

Hearth Method:

1. Follow Steps 1-4 in the recipe above.
2. Follow Steps 2 and 3 in the recipe on page 182.

Fritters

"Flat-jacks, or fritters, do not differ from pancakes, only in being mixed softer. The same ingredients are used in about the same quantities; only most people prefer to have no sweetening put in them, because they generally have butter, sugar, and nutmeg put on them, after they are done. Excepting for company, the nutmeg can be well dispensed with. They are not to be boiled in fat, like pancakes; the spider or griddle should be well greased, and the cakes poured on as large as you want them, when it is quite hot; when it gets brown on one side, to be turned over upon the other. Fritters are better to be baked quite thin. Either flour, Indian, or rye, is good."

2 eggs
1 cup milk
1½ cups flour or cornmeal, measured after sifting
1 tsp. baking powder
½ tsp. cinnamon
⅛ tsp. cloves
¼ tsp. salt
1 tsp. nutmeg
5 tbl. sugar
Fat to grease skillet
Butter

Modern Method:

1. Beat eggs and milk together.
2. Sift flour with baking powder, cinnamon, cloves, salt, and 2 tbl. sugar. Stir quickly into egg and milk mixture.
3. Preheat skillet or griddle. When hot, grease, and drop 2-3 tbl. batter for each fritter onto skillet. Turn when first side is browned. Grease griddle lightly after every two or three batches.

4. Combine 3 tbl. sugar and nutmeg. Serve fritter with butter and nutmeg-sugar.

Hearth Method:

1. Follow Steps 1 and 2 in the recipe above.
2. Follow Steps 3 and 4 in the recipe above, using a hanging skillet.

Yield: 16-18

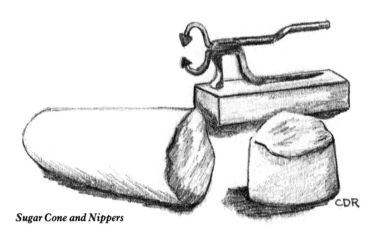

Sugar Cone and Nippers

Pancakes

"Pancakes should be made of half a pint of milk, three great spoon-fuls of sugar, one or two eggs, a tea-spoonful of dissolved pearlash, spiced with cinnamon, or cloves, a little salt, rose-water, or lemon-brandy, just as you happen to have it . Flour should be stirred in till the spoon moves round with difficulty. If they are thin, they are apt to soak fat. Have the fat in your skillet boiling hot, and drop them in with a spoon. Let them cook till thoroughly brown. The fat which is left is good to shorten other cakes. The more fat they are cooked in, the less they soak."

2 eggs
1 cup milk
2 cups flour, measured after sifting
3 tbl. sugar
1 tsp. baking powder
½ tsp. cinnamon
⅛ tsp. cloves
¼ tsp. salt
Fat for deep frying

Modern Method:

1. Beat eggs and add milk. Set aside.
2. In a large mixing bowl combine flour, sugar, baking powder, spices, and salt.
3. Pour milk and egg mixture into center of dry ingredients and stir quickly.
4. Heat oil or fat for frying in a deep skillet or deep fat fryer, 375° in an electric fryer. The fat is hot enough when a small pinch of dough dropped in rises to the surface of the fat immediately.
5. Drop batter into the fat by tablespoons, leaving enough room for the pancakes to swell as they cook. When one

side is browned, about 5 minutes, turn to brown other side.
6. Drain on paper towels. Serve warm with butter and maple syrup.

Hearth Method:

1. Follow Steps 1-3 in the recipe above.
2. Follow Step 4 in the recipe above, using a hanging skillet.
3. Pull skillet forward to drop batter into the fat. Push back over fire to brown, about 5 minutes. Turn pancake to brown other side.
4. Follow Step 6 in the recipe above.

Yield: 48

There were such nice waffles (in the picnic basket) as nobody could bake but Grandma and such tender cold tongue, and dainty delicate slices of boiled ham and such nice cakes and comfits.

Ellen Louise Chandler, "A Husking Party at Ryefield" *This That and The Other* (Boston, 1854)

Apple Pancakes

"One pint of sour milk, a tea-spoonful of saleratus, a tea-cup of fine Indian meal, a tea-cup of molasses, three sweet apples chopped fine and mixed in, and flour enough to make the right thickness to drop from a spoon. Have your fat boiling hot. Cook till they slip from the fork."

2 cups sour milk or 1¾ cups fresh milk with 2 tbl. lemon juice
¾ cup cornmeal
2 apples
1 tsp. baking soda
¾ cup molasses
2-2½ cups sifted flour
Fat for deep frying
Butter

Tea Kettle

Modern Method:

1. Mix cornmeal and milk.
2. Chop apples and stir into milk and cornmeal. Add molasses and baking soda.
3. Stir in flour.
4. Heat fat for frying in deep skillet or deep fat fryer, 375° in an electric fryer. The fat is hot enough when a small pinch of dough dropped in rises to the surface of the fat immediately.
5. Drop batter into the fat by tablespoonfuls, leaving enough room for the pancakes to swell as they cook. When one side is browned, about 3-5 minutes, turn pancake to brown other side.
6. Drain on paper towels. Serve warm with butter.

Hearth Method:

1. Follow steps 1-3 in the recipe above.
2. Heat fat in hanging skillet and follow step 4 in the recipe above. Pull away from fire when adding batter or turning pancakes. Turn when browned on first side.
3. Follow step 6 in the recipe above.

Yield: 5 dozen

Cider Cake

"Cider cake is very good, to be baked in small loaves. One pound and a half of flour, half a pound of sugar, quarter of a pound of butter, half a pint of cider, one teaspoonful of pearlash; spice to your taste. Bake till it turns easily in the pans. I should think about half an hour."

½ cup butter
½ cup sugar
2 eggs
3 cups flour
1 tsp. baking powder
½ tsp. nutmeg
¼ tsp. cinnamon
1 cup cider

Modern Method:

1. Cream butter and sugar. Add eggs and blend well.
2. Sift flour, baking powder, and spices.
3. Add flour mixture and cider alternately to butter mixture, beginning with flour and stirring well after each addition. Batter will be stiff.
4. Pour into two greased 5″ x 9″ loaf pans or two 8-inch or 9-inch pie plates.
5. Bake 50-55 minutes at 350°.

Hearth Method:

1. Follow Steps 1-3 in the recipe above.
2. Pour into two greased ceramic or cast-iron loaf pans 8-inch or 9-inch pottery pie plates.
3. Bake 55 minutes in moderate bake oven, or bake 45 minutes in preheated Dutch oven with coals on lid and beneath.

Yield: two 8-inch or 9-inch rounds, or two 5″ x 9″ loaves

190

Short Cake

"If you have sour milk, or butter-milk, it is well to make it into short cakes for tea. Rub in a very small bit of shortening, or three table-spoonfuls of cream, with the flour; put in a tea-spoonful of strong dissolved pearlash, into your sour milk, and mix your cake pretty stiff, to bake in the spider, on a few embers. When people have to buy butter and lard, short cakes are not economical food. A half-pint of flour will make a cake large enough to cover a common plate. Knead it stiff enough to roll well, to bake in a plate or in a spider. It should bake as quick as it can and not burn. The first side should stand longer to the fire than the last."

¼ cup butter, shortening, or sour milk
2 cups flour
1 tsp. baking soda
¾ cup sour milk or buttermilk

Modern Method:

1. Blend butter, shortening, or sour milk with 1¾ cups flour.
2. Stir soda into sour milk or buttermilk and mix with flour mixture. Batter will be sticky.
3. Sprinkle remaining ¼ cup of flour over a board and knead for less than a minute. Roll dough to the size of an 8-inch or 9-inch pie plate and place it in the plate.
4. Bake in 425° oven for 10-12 minutes.

Hearth Method:

1. Follow Steps 1-3 in the recipe above, rolling dough to the size of the spider or plate to be used.
2. Bake in a preheated spider over hot coals. After 5 minutes, turn and bake 3-4 minutes on the other side. Or bake on a pie plate or flat plate on a trivet over coals, turning after 5-6 minutes and cooking 3-4 minutes on the other side.

Yield: one 8-inch or 9-inch cake

Indian Cake

"Indian cake, or bannock is sweet and cheap food. Two cups of Indian meal, one table-spoonful molasses, two cups milk, a little salt, a handful flour, a little saleratus, mixed up thin, and poured into a buttered bake-kettle, hung over the fire uncovered, until you can bear your finger upon it, and then set down before the fire. Bake half an hour. A little stewed pumpkin, scalded with the meal improves the cake. Bannock split and dipped in butter makes very nice toast."

1½ cups cornmeal
1½ cups very hot milk
½ cup cooked pumpkin, optional
1 tbl. molasses
1 tsp. salt
¼ cup flour
2 tsp. baking soda
¼ cup butter or lard
Butter

Modern Method:

1. Scald cornmeal by pouring hot milk over it gradually, stirring to blend. Stir in cooked pumpkin, if desired. When the milk is absorbed, and mixture has cooled, continue with the recipe.
2. Stir molasses into scalded cornmeal. Add flour, salt, and baking soda.
3. Preheat a 9-inch cast-iron skillet and melt butter or lard in it on top of stove. Pour in batter and stir constantly while it cooks. In 5 minutes or less it will be firm.
4. Remove from heat immediately. Spread the batter evenly in the skillet and smooth the top with the back of a spoon.
5. Bake in the oven, at 350°, for ½ hour, no more.
6. Serve warm or after it cools, split and toast. Serve with butter.

Hearth Method:

1. Follow Steps 1 and 2 in the recipe above.
2. Preheat hanging skillet and melt butter or lard. Pour in batter and stir constantly while it cooks. In about 10-15 minutes it will be firm.
3. Follow Step 4 in the recipe above.
4. Prop skillet against a brick or other heavy object so that the dough is facing the heat of the fire to bake for ½ hour.
5. Follow Step 6 in the recipe above.

Churn

Washington Cake

"Beat six eggs very light; one pound of butter; a pound of sugar. Beat separately and then mix together. Add one pound and a half of flour; a pint of rich milk or cream a little sour; a glass of wine; a powdered nutmeg; a spoonful of cinnamon; and lastly, a small teaspoonful of saleratus. Bake in tins or small pans in a brisk oven, and if wrapped in a thick cloth will keep soft for a week."

¾ cup butter
1 cup sugar
3 eggs
¼ cup wine
2½-3 cups flour, measured after sifting
1 tsp. baking soda
2 tsp. nutmeg
1½ tsp. cinnamon
½ pt. heavy cream

Modern Method:

1. Cream butter and sugar until light.
2. Beat eggs, add wine. Combine with butter and sugar mixture.
3. Sift together flour, baking soda, and spices.
4. Add one third of the flour mixture and half of the cream, then add one third of the flour mixture and the remaining cream, and then add the remaining flour mixture, blending well after each addition.
5. Grease two 8-inch round cake pans, pour in batter and bake for 45 minutes, or use a tube pan and bake for 70 minutes at 350°.

Hearth Method:

1. Follow Steps 1-4 in the recipe above.

194

2. Put batter in two 9-inch pottery pie plates or two round, straight-sided ovenproof dishes of 8-9 inches in diameter. Bake for 1¼ hours in a moderate bake oven.

Yield: two 8-inch or 9-inch layers, or one tube cake

After the oration came another national salute —
thirteen guns, one for each of the original states . . . a
feu de joie from the old flint lock muskets of the militia
and then an attack upon the bread and cheese & rum
punch provided by the committee.

Francis M. Thompson, *History of Greenfield, Shire Town of Franklin
County* (Greenfield, 1904)

Jumbles

"Sift a pound of flour into a large pan. Cut up a pound of butter into a pound of powdered white sugar, and stir them into a cream. Beat six eggs till very light, and then pour them all at once into the pan of flour; next add the butter and sugar, with a large table-spoonful of mixed mace and cinnamon, two grated nutmegs, and the juice of two lemons, or a wine glass of rose water. When all the ingredients are in, stir the mixture very hard with a broad knife. Having floured your hands and spread some flour on the paste-board, make the dough into long rolls all of equal size and form them into rings by joining the two ends very nicely. Lay them on buttered tins and bake them in a quick oven from five to ten min-utes. Grate sugar over them when cool."

1 cup butter
2 cups powdered sugar or 1 cup granulated sugar, pow-
    dered in blender or with a mortar and pestle
3 eggs
1 tbl. rose water or lemon extract
2 cups whole-wheat flour, measured after sifting
1 tbl. nutmeg
½ tsp. mace
½ tsp. cinnamon
1 cup powdered sugar

Modern Method:

1. Cream butter and sugar.
2. Beat eggs and rose water or lemon extract until light and blend into butter and sugar mixture.
3. Sift flour and spices, add to egg mixture, stirring until blended. If dough is very soft, chill for 2 hours.
4. On a lightly floured board, roll dough with the palm of your hand into strips of ¼ to ½ inch in diameter. Cut into 6-inch lengths and form into a circle. Place 1 inch apart on

a lightly greased baking sheet to allow for expansion.

5. Bake 8-10 minutes in 375° oven.
6. When cool, sift powdered sugar over jumbles or shake a few cookies at a time in a bag with powdered sugar.

Hearth Method:

1. Follow Steps 1-4 in the recipe above.
2. If using metal cookie sheets in a brick oven, place on trivets. Bake in a hot oven for 8-10 minutes. Small cakes with a short cooking time can be baked more easily in a Dutch oven on a pottery pie plate. Change coals after every second batch.
3. Follow Step 6 in the recipe above.

Yield: 3-4 dozen

Herb and Spice Box

Wafers

"Dry the flour well which you intend to use, mix a little pounded sugar and finely pounded mace with it, then make it into a thick batter with cream; butter the wafer irons, let them be hot, put a teaspoonful of batter into them, so bake them carefully, and roll them off the iron with a stick.

"If you are preparing for company, fill up the hollow of the wafers with whipt cream, and stop up the two ends with preserved strawberries or with any other small sweetmeat."

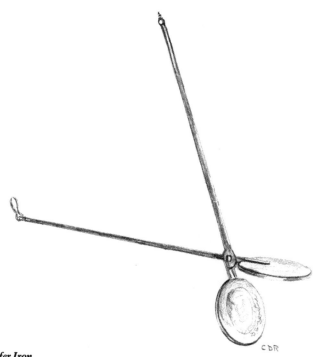

Wafer Iron

¼ lb. butter
4 eggs
½ cup sugar
½ tsp. mace
1¼ cups sifted flour
2 cups whipped cream
Strawberry preserves, frozen whole strawberries or other
    fruits
Large pat of butter

Modern Method:

1. Preheat pizzelle or krumkake iron according to manufacturer's instructions while batter is mixed.
2. Melt ¼ lb. butter.
3. Beat eggs; add sugar, mace, and melted butter.
4. Add flour and blend.
5. Remove iron from fire, place on pads or towels to protect
   table. Wrap a lump of butter in a clean cloth and brush
   lightly over both sides of iron to grease it.
6. Place 1 tbl. of batter in center of iron, and leave for about
   30 seconds. Remove immediately. Two wafers can be
   made before iron has to be reheated.
7. While still warm and pliable, roll wafers into cylinders
   using the handle of a wooden spoon. Allow to cool. Spoon
   whipped cream into hollow and garnish with fruit or
   preserves.

Hearth Method:

1. Preheat wafer iron in glowing coals while batter is mixed.
2. To mix, cook and serve follow Steps 2-7 in recipe above.

Yield: 30-36 wafers

Macaroons

"Beat to a froth the whites of 8 eggs, then add 2 lb. finely pounded and sifted loaf sugar, one pound of blanched sweet almonds, which must be pounded to a paste with rose water. Beat all these together till they become a thick paste, then drop it from a spoon upon a buttered tin. Place the drops a little apart as they may spread. Bake them about 10 minutes in a moderate oven. Cocoanut cakes may be made in the same manner substituting for the pounded almonds ½ lb. finely grated cocoanut."

2⅔ cups ground almonds
1 tsp. rose water or vanilla extract
2 cups granulated sugar
8 egg whites
2 cups sifted rye flour

Modern Method:

1. Grind almonds to a paste with rose water or vanilla.
2. Grind sugar in blender or with mortar and pestle if available. Beat egg whites and gradually add sugar to them.
3. Stir in flour and almond paste.
4. Drop batter by teaspoonfuls one inch apart on buttered cookie sheet. Bake 10 minutes in 350° oven.

Hearth Method:

1. Follow Steps 1-3 in the recipe above.
2. To bake in Dutch oven, drop batter by teaspoonfuls one inch apart on buttered pie plate. Bake 8-10 minutes. Change coals after every second batch.

COCONUT MACAROONS:

Substitute 2½ cups flaked coconut for almonds; reduce flour to 1 cup. Omit Step 1 and use flour and coconut flakes in Step 3.

Yield: 6 dozen

200

Bread, Yeast, &c.

Bread

*"It is more difficult to give rules for making bread than for any-
thing else; it depends so much on judgment and experience. In
summer, bread should be mixed with cold water; during a chilly
damp spell, the water should be slightly warm; in severe cold
weather it should be mixed quite warm and set in a warm place
during the night. If your yeast is new and lively, a small quantity
will make the bread rise; if it be old and heavy, it will take more.
In these things I believe wisdom must be gained by a few
mistakes."*

Yeast

*"Those who make their own bread should make yeast too. When
bread is nearly out, always think whether yeast is in readiness;
for it takes a day and night to prepare it. One handful of hops,
with two or three handsful of malt and rye bran, should be boiled
fifteen or twenty minutes, in two quarts of water, then strained,
hung on to boil again, and thickened with half a pint of rye and
water stirred up quite thick, and a little molasses; boil it a minute
or two, and then take it off to cool. When just about lukewarm,
put in a cupful of good lively yeast, and set it in a cool place in
summer, and warm place in winter. If it is too warm when you
put in the old yeast, all the spirit will be killed."*

1 cup dried hops
2-3 cups whole-wheat or rye flour
2 qt. water
½ cup rye flour
1 tbl. molasses
1 cup water
1 pkg. commercial yeast or 1 cup reserved yeast from pre-
vious batch

Modern Method:

1. In a large pot, combine hops, flour, and water. Bring to a boil over high heat and cook for 2 minutes.
2. Strain the water off and return it to the cooking pot.
3. Make up a thick paste of rye flour, molasses and water. Stir this into the liquid in the pot. Bring to the boil, stir, and boil again briefly. Remove from heat to cool.
4. When lukewarm, stir in 1 pkg. commercial yeast or 1 cup reserved yeast.
5. Store loosely covered in a glass container in a cool place. It is ready to use in 24 hours.

Hearth Method:

1. Follow Steps 1-3 in the recipe above, using a large hanging kettle over a hot fire.
2. Follow Steps 4 and 5 in the recipe above.

Flour Bread

"*Flour bread should have a sponge set the night before. The sponge should be soft enough to pour; mixed with water, warm or cold, according to the temperature of the weather. One gill of lively yeast is enough to put into sponge for two loaves. I should judge about three pints of sponge would be right for two loaves. The warmth of the place in which the sponge is set, should be determined by the coldness of the weather. If your sponge looks frothy in the morning; it is a sign your bread will be good; if it does not rise, stir in a little more emptings; if it rises too much, taste of it, to see if it has any acid taste; if so, put in a tea-spoonful of pearlash when you mould in your flour; be sure the pearlash is well dissolved in water; if there are little lumps, your bread will be full of bitter spots. About an hour before your oven is ready, stir in flour into your sponge till it is stiff enough to lay on a well floured board or table. Knead it up pretty stiff, and put it into well greased pans, and let it stand in a cool or warm place, according to the weather. . . . Common sized loaves will bake in three quarters of an hour. If they slip easily in the pans, it is a sign they are done.*"

4-5 cups wheat flour, measured after sifting
2 pkg. dry yeast, dissolved in 2 cups warm water and 1 tsp.
   sugar, or 1 cup homemade yeast (recipe on page 202)
   and 1 cup water

Modern Method:

1. Beat together 2 cups flour and liquid yeast by hand or for 2-3 minutes with electric mixer. This is the sponge.
2. Let rise overnight in refrigerator. Bowl should be covered with a cloth.
3. Add 2-3 cups sifted flour to form a soft dough. Knead 10 minutes on board sprinkled with ¼ cup flour.
4. Divide dough in half. Grease two 8-inch or 9-inch pie plates or two 5″ x 9″ tin or ceramic loaf pans. Shape round

loaves so that the dough covers the bottom of the pan. For rectangular loaves, roll out or flatten the divided dough into two 9-inch-long cylinders, and fit them from end to end in each loaf pan.

5. Let dough rise two hours or more until doubled in bulk.
6. Preheat oven to 400°. Put bread in oven and reduce heat to 375°. Bake loaves for 50 minutes.
7. Remove from pans and cool.

Hearth Method:

1. Follow Step 1 in the recipe above, beating by hand.
2. Follow Step 2 in the recipe above, letting dough rise 1½ hours beside coals on the hearth.
3. Follow Steps 3 and 4 in the recipe above. (Do not use tin loaf pans.)
4. Let dough rise until doubled in bulk. This is a good time to begin to preheat the bake oven, as both will require about 2 hours.
5. Bake bread in hot oven for 45-50 minutes.
6. Remove from pans and cool.

Yield: two 8-inch or 9-inch rounds, or two 5" x 9" loaves

If you have breakfasted early, it will be well to put some ginger bread nuts or biscuits into your satchel, as you may become very hungry before dinner.

— Eliza Leslie, *The Behaviour Book*, Philadelphia, 1854

Three-Grain Bread

"Some people like one third Indian in their flour. Others like one third rye; and some think the nicest of all bread is one third Indian, one third rye and one third flour made according to the directions for flour bread.

"When Indian is used it should be salted, and scalded before the other meal is put in."

4 cups boiling water
2 cups cornmeal
2 tsp. salt
½ cup liquid yeast (recipe on page 202) or 2 pkg. dry yeast
    dissolved in ½ cup water and 1 tsp. sugar
2¼ cups rye flour
2 cups wheat flour, measured after sifting

Modern Method:

1. To make sponge, pour boiling water over cornmeal and salt in a large mixing bowl. Let it sit until the water is absorbed. Stir in yeast and 1 cup of rye flour. To set the sponge, cover the bowl and let it rest overnight in the

Toaster   C.DR

refrigerator. The sponge will probably look flat, but the yeast will have worked.

2. To the sponge, add the wheat flour and 1 cup rye flour.
3. Knead for 10 minutes on a board sprinkled with rye flour. Divide dough in half. Grease two 8-inch or 9-inch pie plates or two 5″ x 9″ tin or ceramic loaf pans. Shape round loaves so that the dough covers the bottom of the pan. For rectangular loaves, roll out or flatten the divided dough into two 9-inch-long cylinders, and fit them from end to end in each loaf pan.
4. Set in a warm place to rise until double in bulk, about 2 hours.
5. Preheat oven to 400°. Put bread in oven and reduce heat to 375°. Bake for 50 minutes.

Hearth Method:

1. Follow Steps 1-3 in the recipe above. Do not use tin or aluminum baking pans.
2. Set in warm place to rise until double in bulk. This is a good time to begin to preheat the bake oven, as both will require about 2 hours.
3. Bake bread in a hot oven for 45-50 minutes.

Yield: two 8-inch or 9-inch rounds, or two 5″ x 9″ loaves

Rolls

"At dinner parties it is customary to have light French rolls instead of pieces of cut bread.

"Warm an ounce of butter in half a pint of milk, then add a spoonful and a half of yeast, and a little salt. Put two pounds of flour in a pan, and mix in the above ingredients. Let it rise an hour — or over night in a cool place; knead it well. Make into seven rolls, and bake them in a quick oven. Add half a teaspoonful of saleratus, just as you put the rolls into the baker."

2 tbl. butter
1 cup milk, at room temperature
1 pkg. yeast or ½ cup homemade yeast (recipe on
    page 202)
1 tsp. salt
4 cups flour
1 tsp. baking soda

Modern Method:

1. Melt butter. Using a large bowl combine butter, milk, yeast, and salt. Mixture will be foamy.
2. Mix in flour and baking soda. Knead for 10 minutes. Cover bowl and leave to rise in a warm place for about an hour or refrigerate overnight.
3. Shape into four rolled loaves or three-dozen finger rolls. Arrange on a greased cookie sheet, leaving room for rolls to expand. Let rise until doubled in bulk.
4. Bake at 400° for 20 minutes.

Hearth Method:

1. Melt butter in a large mixing bowl set on a trivet over coals. When butter has melted remove from fire. Add milk, yeast, and salt. Mixture will be foamy.

2. Follow Step 2 in the recipe above.
3. Shape into four rolled loaves or three-dozen finger rolls, and place on oven-proof pottery or cast-iron baking sheets, leaving room for rolls to expand. Let rise two hours or until doubled in bulk.
4. Bake in a hot brick oven or preheated Dutch oven for 20 minutes.

Yield: four loaves or three dozen finger rolls

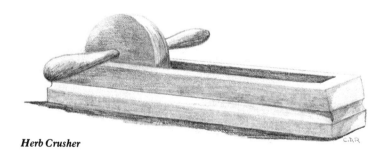

Herb Crusher

Rusks

"*Beat seven eggs well and mix with half a pint of new milk, in which has been melted four ounces of butter; add to it a quarter of a pint of yeast, and three ounces of sugar and put them, by degrees, into as much flour as will make a very light paste, rather like a batter; and let it rise before the fire half an hour; then add some more flour to make it a little stiffer, but not stiff. Work it well and divide it into small loaves or cakes, about four to six inches wide, and flatten them. When baked and cold, since them the thickness of rusks, and put them in the oven to brown a little.*

"*Note. The cakes, when first baked, eat deliciously buttered for tea; or with caraways to eat cold.*"

¼ lb. butter
1 cup milk
7 eggs
6 tbl. sugar
1 pkg. yeast dissolved in ½ cup warm water or ½ cup
    homemade yeast (recipe page 202)
6-7 cups flour, wheat and rye in any proportion

Modern Method:

1. Melt butter and combine with milk.
2. Beat eggs until light, add to milk and butter mixture, sugar, and yeast.
3. Stir in 3 cups of flour and beat for 2-3 minutes. Cover the bowl and set the sponge in a warm place for an hour or more, or refrigerate overnight.
4. To prepare for cooking, add remaining flour so that the dough is no longer sticky.
5. Divide dough in half and make two long rolls. Cut each into twelve slices. Flatten out these slices so that they are 3-4 inch in diameter, resembling an English muffin.
6. Preheat and grease a griddle or heavy skillet. Put three or four cakes on the cooking surface. Cook for 7 minutes, turn and press down. Cook 7-8 minutes on the other side.
7. Split and serve immediately, with butter and preserves, if desired. After they have cooled, they may be split and toasted. (Use instead of toast for the roasted cheese recipe on page 102.)

Hearth Method:

1. Follow Step 1 in the recipe above, melt butter in a pan set on a trivet over coals.
2. Follow Steps 2-5 in the recipe above.
3. Preheat a hanging skillet, grease it and place three or four cakes on the cooking surface. Cook about 7 minutes, watching that they do not burn. Turn and press down. Cook 7-8 minutes on the other side.
4. Follow Step 7 in the recipe above.

Yield: 2 dozen

Rice Bread

"Boil a pint of rice soft; add a pint of leaven; then three quarts of the flour; put it to rise in a tin or earthen vessel until it has risen sufficiently; divide it into three parts; then bake it as other bread, and you will have three large loaves."

1 cup rice
2 qt. water
1 pkg. dry yeast or ½ cup homemade yeast (recipe on page 202)
2 tsp. sugar or molasses
1 tsp. salt
6-7 cups flour, measured after sifting

Modern Method:

1. Cook rice until soft in water. Drain excess water, reserving 1 cup if packaged yeast is used. Cool rice and liquid until lukewarm.
2. Dissolve yeast in reserved liquid to which sugar or molasses has been added. If homemade yeast is used, add sugar or molasses.
3. Add rice, salt, and flour, blending to form a soft dough.
4. Knead for 10 minutes. Cover and let rise for 1½-2 hours.
5. Divide dough in half. Place in two ungreased 5″ x 9″ loaf pans or two 8-inch or 9-inch pie plates. Let rise 1 hour.
6. Bake at 350° for ¾ hour.

Hearth Method:

1. Follow Step 1 in the recipe above, using a hanging kettle over a moderate fire.
2. Follow Steps 2-5 in the recipe above.
3. Bake bread in hot brick oven for 45-50 minutes, or use preheated Dutch ovens with coals on lid and below.

Yield: two 8-inch or 9-inch rounds, or two 5″ x 9″ loaves

Preserves, etc.

Preserves

"Economical people will seldom use preserves, except for sickness. They are unhealthy, and useless to those who are well. A pound of sugar to a pound of fruit is the rule for all preserves. The sugar should be melted over a fire moderate enough not to scorch it. When melted, it should be skimmed clean, and the fruit dropped in to simmer till it is soft. Plums and things of which the skin is liable to be broken, do better to be put in little jars, with their weight of sugar and the jars set in a kettle of boiling water till the fruit is done. See the water is not so high as to boil into the jars.

"When you put the preserves in jars, lay a white paper, thoroughly wet with brandy, flat upon the surface of the preserves, and cover them carefully from the air. If they begin to mould, scald them by setting them in the oven till boiling hot. Glass is much better than earthen for preserves: they are not half as apt to ferment."

[Like Mrs. Child, we have reservations about recommending open-hearth preserves. Our difficulties are not with the cost of the sugar that makes them uneconomical, although that is certainly a factor. Rather, they should not be attempted without adequate tin-lined cooking utensils when cooking fruit directly over heat. Secondly, with methods of canning and refrigeration developed after the middle of the nineteenth century, there is no need to risk storage situations that would invite mold.

Mrs. Child's directions for plum preserves at the hearth call for a boiling water bath suspended over the hearth, rather than in a pressure canner, which would be recommended today. Follow the manufacturer's instructions.— *Ed.*]

Currant Jelly

"Currant jelly is a useful thing for sickness. If it be necessary to wash your currants, be sure they are thoroughly drained, or your jelly will be thin. Break them up with a pestle, and squeeze them through a cloth. Put a pint of clean sugar to a pint of juice and boil it slowly, till it becomes ropy. Great care must be taken not to do it too fast; it is spoiled by being scorched. It should be frequently skimmed while simmering. If currants are put in a jar, and kept in boiling water, and cooked before they are strained, they are more likely to keep a long time without fermenting."

Freshly picked currants on their stems
Sugar
Paraffin

Modern and Hearth Method:

1. Wash currants, put them into a heavy stainless-steel, enameled, or tin-lined pan and heat slowly until liquid forms. Then cook over a higher heat until fruit loses its color.
2. To strain the currants, use a jelly bag, made of several thicknesses of cheesecloth. Wet the jelly bag and put the cooked fruit in. Let the liquid drip into a bowl or pan, but do not squeeze the bag, or the jelly will be bitter.
3. Return liquid to heavy cooking pan, and for every cup of juice, add a cup of sugar. Cook slowly to 220°.
4. Ladle into sterilized jars and seal with paraffin.

Yield: 8 oz. jelly for each cup of juice and cup of sugar

Apple Sauce

"Pare and quarter the apples — if not tart, stew them in cider — if tart enough, stew them in water. When stewed soft, put in a small piece of butter and sweeten it to the taste, with sugar. The kind of sauce will keep good several months. It makes very good plain pies, with the addition of a little cinnamon or cloves."

½ gal. cider
3 lb. apples
Sugar
Butter

Modern Method:

1. Simmer cider until reduced by half and syrupy.
2. Peel the apples, remove core and cut into quarters.
3. Stew apples in reduced cider until soft.
4. Add butter and sugar to taste.
5. Serve applesauce by itself, or use in the recipe for Apple Pie on page 162, or Marlborough Pudding on page 165.

Hearth Method:

1. Follow Step 1 in the recipe above, using a large hanging pot.
2. Follow Steps 2-5 in the recipe above.

Yield: 2 quarts

Applesauce is always proper to accompany roasted pork — this with potatoes, mashed or plain, mashed turnips and pickles is good.

— Sarah J. Hale, *The Way to Live Well and Be Well While We Live,* (Philadelphia, 1839)

Cranberry Sauce

"To make cranberry sauce, nothing more is necessary than to stew the cranberries till soft; then stir in sugar and molasses to sweeten it. Let the sugar scald in it a few minutes. Strain it if you like — it is very good without straining."

1 lb. cranberries
2-3 cups sweetening, sugar or molasses or a combination

Modern Method:

1. Simmer cranberries over low heat, until soft, approximately 12-15 minutes.
2. Straining is optional. To remove seeds and skins, use a food mill or strain pulp through a very coarse strainer. Reheat before adding sugar or molasses. Use only about 2 cups of sugar or molasses if skins and seeds have been discarded.
3. Stir sugar or molasses into hot sauce and remove from heat when completely melted, about 2-3 minutes. Serve hot or cold.

Hearth Method:

1. Follow Step 1 in the recipe above, using a large hanging kettle over a slow fire.
2. Follow Steps 2 and 3 in the recipe above.

Yield: 6 cups

Catsup

"The best sort of catsup is made from tomatoes. The vegetables should be squeezed up in the hand, salt put to them, and set by for twenty-four hours. After being passed through a sieve, cloves, allspice, pepper, mace, garlic, and whole mustard-seed should be added. It should be boiled down one third, and bottled after it is cool. No liquid is necessary, as the tomatoes are very juicy. A good deal of salt and spice is necessary to keep the catsup well. It is delicious with roast meat; and a cupful adds much to the richness of soup and chowder. The garlic should be taken out before it is bottled."

Tomatoes
Salt
Whole cloves
Whole allspice berries
Mace
Garlic
Pepper
Mustard seed

Modern Method:

1. Chop and crush fresh, ripe tomatoes. For every four good-sized tomatoes, sprinkle 2 tablespoons of salt. Cover and refrigerate for 24 hours.
2. Puree tomatoes in a blender or food mill and measure.
3. To each quart of puree, add four whole cloves, four whole allspice berries, ⅛ teaspoon mace, 1 teaspoon pepper, 1 garlic clove, and ½ teaspoon mustard seed.
4. Simmer slowly in a pan to blend flavors and reduce by one third to one half. This will take approximately 2-2½ hours, depending on the quantity and kind of tomatoes used and the type of pan. (It will take less time if an uncovered electric skillet is used.) The catsup will be brown and

is ready when the liquid has boiled away. Remove garlic before packing in sterilized pint jars. Seal according to manufacturer's directions.

Hearth Method:

1. Follow Steps 1-4 in the recipe above, using a tin-lined pan to reduce the ingredients.

Yield: 1 pint per 4 large tomatoes

Beanpot

Pickling to Preserve Vegetables

"Cucumbers should be in weak brine three or four days after they are picked; then they should be put in a tin or wooden pail of clean water, and kept slightly warm in the kitchen corner for two or three days. Then take as much vinegar as you think your pickle jar will hold; scald it with pepper, allspice, mustard-seed, flag-root, horseradish, &c., if you happen to have them; half of them will spice the pickles very well. Throw in a bit of alum as big as a walnut; this serves to make pickles hard. Skim the vinegar clean, and pour it scalding hot upon the cucumbers. Brass vessels are not healthy for preparing anything acid. Red cabbages need no other pickling than scalding, spiced vinegar poured upon them, and suffered to remain eight or ten days before you eat them. Some people think it improves them to keep them in salt and water twenty-four hours before they are pickled."

Brine (6 tbl. salt to a qt. of water)
1 qt. vinegar
2 tbl. whole peppercorns
1 tbl. whole allspice
1 tbl. whole mustard seed
Cucumbers, washed and packed in large jar, or red cabbage, washed, shredded, and packed in large jar, or green tomatoes, washed and packed in large jar

Modern and Hearth Method:

1. Make brine to soak cucumbers overnight.
2. In morning, simmer vinegar with spices for 10 minutes in a stainless steel or enamelled pot.
3. Pour vinegar immediately over the cucumbers, cabbage, or tomatoes, packed in stoneware, lead-free pottery, or glass jars.
4. Cover and let set a week or so in a cool place before eating.

The American Citron

"Take the rind of a large watermelon not too ripe, cut it into small pieces. Take two pounds of loaf sugar; one pint of water and put it all into a kettle, let it boil gently for four hours, then put it into pots for use."

1 small round watermelon or ⅓ of a very large oval watermelon
4 cups sugar
2 cups water

Modern Method:

1. Chop watermelon rind into ½-inch cubes.
2. Place rinds, sugar and water in a large heavy pan. Bring to a boil, then turn down heat and simmer 3-4 hours until rind is tender and a thick syrup has formed.
3. If not to be used immediately, pack in sterilized pint jars and seal according to manufacturer's directions.
4. Use in the recipe for Wedding Cake on page 178 or for other fruitcakes, or serve as relish.

Hearth Method:

1. Follow Steps 1 and 2 in the recipe above, using a small tin-lined or enamelled hanging kettle over a slow fire.
2. Follow Steps 3 and 4 in the recipe above.

Yield: 3-4 pints

Dried Pumpkin and Apples

"Some people cut pumpkin, string it and dry it like apples."

DRIED PUMPKIN:
1 pumpkin
Needle
String to extend between nails on either side of hearth or other warm, dry place

Modern and Hearth Method:

1. Cut pumpkin in half and scoop out seeds.
2. Cut pumpkin into vertical strips at ½-inch intervals. Peel the strips. Cut into 2-3-inch lengths.
3. Thread the needle with the string, and string the pumpkin. It will be heavy, but as it dries, the large squares will shrivel. When dried, pack in bags and store in cool, dry place.
4. To reconstitute, soak the pumpkin pieces overnight. Stew them covered in water and proceed with the recipe for Pumpkin Pie on page 156 or Indian Cake on page 192, or any other recipe calling for pumpkin.

DRIED APPLES:
Apples
Needle
String to extend between nails on either side of the hearth or other warm, dry place

Modern and Hearth Method:

1. Peel and core whole apples. Slice into rings.
2. Insert string through the hole in the apple rings. Hang to dry. Apples should feel like cardboard when thoroughly dried.

3. When dry, store in bags in a cool, dry place.
4. When ready to use, soak apples in hot water for 2 hours, and proceed with recipe for Apple Pie on page 162, or any other recipe calling for apples. Dried apples also make delicious snacks.

To Preserve Apples for the Year Round

"Put them in casks in layers of dry sand. Let the sand be perfectly dry, and each layer being covered keeps them from the air, from moisture, from frost, and from perishing, as the sand absorbs their moisture, which generally perishes them. Pippins have often been kept in this manner until mid-summer, and were as fresh then as when put in."

Modern and Hearth Methods:

1. Store apples in sand in boxes or barrels. Store packed containers in a cool, dry cellar which does not freeze or get too warm. Will keep up to one year. Check frequently and remove spoiled apples. Use up when most apples show signs of spoilage.

Excellent Lemonade

"Take one gallon of water, put to it the juice of ten good lemons, and the zests of six of them likewise, then add to this one pound of sugar, and mix it well together, strain it through a fine strainer and put it in ice to cool. This will be a most delicious and fine lemonade."

2 qt. water
Juice of 5 lemons
Grated rind of 3 lemons
1 cup sugar

Modern and Hearth Method:

1. Mix ingredients together.
2. Strain and chill.

Servings: 4

Raspberry Shrub

"Raspberry shrub mixed with water is a pure, delicious drink for summer; and in a country where raspberries are abundant, it is good economy to make it answer instead of Port and Catalonia wine. Put raspberries in a pan, and scarcely cover them with strong vinegar. Add a pint of sugar to a pint of juice; (of this you can judge by first trying your pan to see how much it holds;) scald it, skim it, and bottle it when cold."

Raspberries
Vinegar
Sugar

Modern and Hearth Method:

1. Cover raspberries with vinegar in a kettle. Do not use cast iron.
2. Simmer until berries are soft.
3. Strain through cheesecloth. Measure juice.
4. For each cup of juice add 1 cup of sugar.
5. Bring juice and sugar just to a boil, skim the top, and ladle into sterilized glass jars. Keep cold or seal jars to store.
6. To serve, mix shrub with water to taste.

Coffee

"Coffee should be put in an iron pot, and dried over a moderate fire for several hours, before it is roasted. It should be put at such a distance from the fire, as to be in no danger of burning. When it has dried three or four hours, set the pot on a hot bed of coals, and stir in constantly, until sufficiently roasted, which is ascertained by biting one of the lightest colored kernels — if it is brittle, the whole is done. Turn it out of the pot immediately, into a box — cover it tight, to keep in the steam. To make good common coffee, allow a table-spoonful of it, when ground, to each pint of water. Turn on the water boiling hot, and boil the coffee in a tin pot, from twenty to twenty-five minutes — if boiled longer, it will not taste fresh and lively. Let it stand, after being taken from the fire, four or five minutes to settle, then turn it off carefully from the gounds, into a coffee-pot or urn. When the coffee is put on the fire to boil, a piece of fish-skin or isinglass, of the size of a nine-pence, should be put in, or else the white and shell of half an egg, to a couple of quarts of coffee."

TO ROAST COFFEE:

Whole coffee beans
Coffee roaster or iron pot with cover

Modern Method:

1. Roast coffee beans in an ungreased roaster or iron skillet over low heat, stirring frequently until they are dark and brittle.
2. Keep roasted beans in a tightly covered container. Grind coffee before using.

Hearth Method:

1. Follow Step 1 in recipe above using a hanging skillet or metal pan on a trivet over hot coals.
2. Follow Step 2 in recipe above.

Coffee Grinder

TO BREW COFFEE:

Ground coffee
Water
Egg white
½ eggshell, crushed

Modern Method:

1. Use a saucepan and put in 1-2 tbl. ground coffee to every 2 cups boiling water. Drop in egg white and washed eggshell.
2. Bring to boil and simmer 20 minutes.
3. Let coffee stand 5 minutes before straining into pot for serving.

Hearth Method:

1. Follow Step 1 in the recipe above, using a tin coffee pot.
2. Put pot on a trivet over hot coals to boil for 20-25 minutes.
3. Follow Step 3 in the recipe above.

Chocolate

"Many people boil chocolate in a coffee-pot; but I think it is better to boil it in a skillet, or something open. A piece of chocolate about as big as a dollar is the usual quantity for a quart of water; but some put in more, and some less. When it boils, pour in as much milk as you like, and let them boil together three or four minutes. It is much richer with the milk boiled into it. Put the sugar in either before or after, as you please. Nutmeg improves it. The chocolate should be scraped fine before it is put into the water."

1 oz. unsweetened chocolate, grated
¼ cup sugar
½ tsp. ground nutmeg, optional
2 cups water
2 cups milk

Modern Method:

1. Melt chocolate in a double boiler. Add sugar and nutmeg, optional, and stir.
2. Add water, and bring to a boil.
3. Add milk, and heat to serving temperature, about 3-4 minutes.
4. Serve hot with grated nutmeg.

Hearth Method:

1. Follow Step 1 in the recipe above, using a skillet over a slow fire.
2. Follow Steps 2-4 in the recipe above.

Yield: 4 cups

Tea

"Young Hyson is supposed to be a more profitable tea than Hyson; but though the quantity to a pound is greater, it has not so much strength. In point of economy, therefore, there is not much difference between them. Hyson tea and Souchong mixed together, half and half, is a pleasant beverage, and is more healthy than green tea alone. Be sure that water boils before it is poured upon tea. A tea-spoonful to each person, and one extra thrown in, is a good rule. Steep ten or fifteen minutes."

Tea, loose
Lemon
Milk
Sugar or honey

Modern and Hearth Method:

1. Before kettle boils, pour some hot water into the teapot to preheat it. As the kettle of water comes to a boil, pour out and discard the water in the teapot.
2. Measure tea and place in pot. Measure 2 tsp. tea per cup desired and add 1 tsp. for the pot.
3. Pour boiling water into the pot over the leaves, allowing ¾ cup per serving.
4. Steep 5 minutes or longer before pouring into cups. Serve with lemon or milk, and sugar or honey to taste.

Servings: 1 per ¾ cup

Appendix

A Visit to Old Sturbridge Village

The ring of the blacksmith's anvil, the click of the shuttle passing through the weaver's loom, the rumble of the ox cart drawing freshly mown hay from the fields—these are some of the sounds you'll hear as you step back in time at the Old Sturbridge Village. Whatever the season, whether the Village is festooned with the pale greens of Spring or blanketed with newly fallen snow, it is always a special place to visit. The pace is leisurely, and you leave the asphalt highways and noise of the twentieth century far behind when you enter this re-created 1830's New England community.

Just a short stroll inside the Village is the Common with two imposing white buildings facing each other down its length. At the east end is the handsome residence built in 1786 for Salem Towne, a man of means accumulated through his farming and mercantile activities. The house furnishings are elegant, and every young girl will wish the canopied bed and star-covered ceiling in the ballroom chamber were her own. At the west end of the Common is the white-steepled 1832 Meetinghouse which was built nearby in the town of Sturbridge. Like virtually all of the buildings at the Village, it was moved to the site. This process began some 40 years ago when Old Sturbridge Village was created and is still continuing as the Village grows.

Around the Common, stroll along unpaved paths to the Asa Knight store, the bank, and the tavern. The illusion of being in the past is heightened with each building you visit. Stop at the Fenno House, interpreted as the dwelling of an elderly widow and her unmarried daughter, and the Fitch House, furnished as the home of the printer whose shop is a short walk away. Pause to observe and talk to the potter, the shoemaker, the cooper, and the blacksmith at work in their shops. At the Pliny Freeman Farm, a complete, working, five-acre farm, you'll see what life was like for the farmer and his family of the early nineteenth century. In all, there are some forty exhibits at the Village, scattered around the Common, and along the country paths and the millpond. Each exhibit is carefully furnished to show how life was lived in the 1830's by people of different means. The Village is situated in a 200-acre landscape, and is surrounded by lovely woods and meadows.

What makes a Village like Sturbridge so realistic and convincing for so many visitors is that as the past is re-created, actual work is being done by historically costumed interpreters. The shoemaker stitches shoes, just the right size for the men and women who will wear them to teach at the Candia Schoolhouse or to sing at worship service in the Meetinghouse. Baskets are made to carry the vegetables grown at the Freeman farm, hold knitting and sewing, or carry wet laundry out to hang in the sunlight. The farmer plows his field with his oxen, using an ox yoke and plow made by the Village woodworkers and blacksmiths.

One visitor recently shared a special moment that took place in the whitewashed kitchen of the Freeman farm. There was a chill in the air, and the farmer was putting on a new blue woolen frock for the very first time before going back to the fields, while his wife looked on. It was a bittersweet moment for her, for she had woven the cloth; she was pleased to see the cloth made up into such an attractive garment, yet she knew that it would soon be dirty. Farm work is like that. For the twentieth-century visitor catching this moment, this seemed like a scene that must have taken place repeatedly 150 years ago.

Join the half-million people who find their way to Sturbridge each year and gain insight about the past with each visit. There are new exhibits each year, and special seasonal demonstrations, such as candlemaking and the militia's Spring Training Day. The Village is a leisurely hour's drive from Hartford or Boston, and three hours from New York City. It is right in the heart of central New England where the Massachusetts Turnpike (I-90) is joined by Interstate 86 from Hartford, New York, and the South. Take Exit 9 off the Turnpike or Exit 3 (Old Sturbridge Village Road) from I-86, and the Village is a short distance away.

The Village is open year round except for Christmas and New Year's Day and on Mondays in the winter.

Sheep graze on the Common at Old Sturbridge Village. The sheep are "back-bred" for fleece and meat characteristics to resemble some of the sheep which would have been found in an 1830's New England village. In the background are the Meetinghouse and the gambrel-roofed Fitch House.

Town meetings are re-enacted twice a year in the Greek Revival Meetinghouse.

The builder of Salem Towne's imposing residence was familiar with William Pain's Practical Builder, *an English carpenter's guide. The elaborate detailing of the ornamented front door is only a sample of the decorative elements taken from Pain which are used throughout the house.*

234

The dining room of the Salem Towne House is fashionably decorated with wallpaper, swagged curtains, a gilded ironstone dinner service in the Imari style and color, and a late 18th-century creamware caster.

The Richardson Parsonage is a mid-18th century lean-to structure, furnished and interpreted as the home of a Congregational minister and his family.

The view from the Fitch House garden includes the Thompson Bank and the Salem Towne House at the right through the trees.

Family life is among the topics discussed at the Fitch House where reproduction children's clothing is exhibited.

From time to time, the parlor of the Fitch House is the setting for re-created meetings of the Charitable Society. The parlor is decorated with wallpaper and simple white curtains. The portraits are of Worcester, Massachusetts printer Southworth Howland (hidden) and his wife Esther Allen Howland, an author of a manual on children's education.

The Common serves as the training ground for the Village militia twice a year. The McClellan Law Office is the one-room building at center. The troops are approaching the 2½-story Asa Knight Store at left.

The storekeeper keeps an assortment of textiles, shoes, ribbons, and notions along with ceramics, hardware, and imported foodstuffs.

The Pliny Freeman Farm is a complete, working farm with field crops, a large kitchen garden, and a variety of livestock. The house was built in 1802.

The farm work re-created at the Pliny Freeman Farm relies on the hardworking team of oxen all year round. They are very special creatures, bred at the Village to resemble the red and white cattle of the 1830's.

The haymows are full of hay, grown, cut, and carted in from the surrounding fields each summer, and stored up to the very rafters until needed during the long winter.

239

At the Freeman Farm the brick oven (left) is preheated in preparation for baking. After the fire has burned for two hours, the oven will be swept out and the pies and breads put in to cook. The ceramics in the cupboard are edged wares commonly found in rural households.

There are three working mills on the Village millpond and stream that utilize waterpower. Here, a delivery is made by ox cart to the Grist Mill. The shingled structure at right is the Carding Mill.

Hand weavers in the early 19th century produced special quality fabrics for their homes and customers. In the foreground strips of a Village-woven coverlet are stitched together. The pattern is "Sixteen Blossoms," a 19th-century document in the collections.

The bottle-shaped kiln was reproduced by Village craftsmen based on archaeological evidence from the Hervey Brooks site in Goshen, Connecticut. It is stacked and fired several times a year.

242

The blacksmith uses the reproduction beam drill to make a hole to hang the fork made at the forge.

The shoemaker is seated at his low bench, using a leg harness to brace the shoe to which he is nailing the sole. Behind him is a stand-up bench, which offers an alternative way to secure the shoe in process. Both benches are reproductions from Village collections.

The Herb Garden is one of several exhibits outside the re-created Village area. Hundreds of culinary, medicinal, and useful plants known to New Englanders a century and a half ago are cultivated in the garden for the enjoyment of today's visitors.

244

Each step in the printing process is a hand operation — setting type, inking, drawing the press, and removing each sheet to hang while the ink dries.

The cooper chops out the stock to be shaved down into staves to make a bucket.
Washtubs, piggins, and barrels are other products of the cooper's trade.

Special events like militia training days are part of the seasonal calendar and provide another chance for visitors to learn more about the past.

The Village provides opportunities to see animals in a natural farm and work setting during four seasons of the year.

Index

Aa

Bb

Ss

Tt

Vv

Ww

Yy

Acknowledgements

For years the hearthside cooks at the Old Sturbridge Village have been learning the recipes and cooking techniques of old New England to present to generations of visitors. This has been the inspiration and incentive for the preparation of the *Old Sturbridge Village Cookbook*, which represents the collaboration of the Village staff in many ways. I am especially indebted to Linda M. Oakley and Anna T. Adams for their help in cooking the recipes at the hearth. Many thanks also to Cynthia Dias-Reid for her illustrations, Robert S. Arnold for his photographs, and Ellen Lind and Nancy Bednarz for their typing and retyping of the recipes. At Globe Pequot Press, another smoothly operating team took over, including Cary Hull, a careful and patient editor.

Many others have made contributions of various kinds, not the least of which has been to sample the recipes as they were cooked. To all, I extend my appreciation.